St. Louis Community College

Library

5801 Wilson Avenue
St. Louis, Missouri 63110

Beyond Marriage
and the
Nuclear Family

Robert Thamm

California State University, San Jose

 Canfield Press San Francisco
A Department of Harper & Row, Publishers, Inc.
New York • Evanston • London

3-3-76

Book design by j. sidonie tillinger
Cover by Richard Cork

Library of Congress Cataloging in Publication Data

Thamm, Robert.
      Beyond marriage and the nuclear family.

      Includes index.
      1. Family.   I. Title.
HQ728.T48   301.42   74-23746
ISBN 0-06-388726-6

75 76 77   10 9 8 7 6 5 4 3 2 1

Contents

Preface

The growing dissatisfaction with monogamous marriage and the middle-class nuclear family is well documented. Since 1890, the rate of increase in divorce has been steady in the United States. As divorce laws continue to be liberalized we can expect to find soaring rates. The U.S. Census Bureau revealed that in 1960 over two million men and women were separated. Desertions, which would add to the number of people left without a family, are not recorded anywhere. A surprising fact related to this is that the number of people living alone is increasing much more rapidly than the sum population of the United States. Between 1960 and 1970, approximately one-third of all new households contained but one person. These figures suggest that an increasing number of people are living outside of marriage and a family. No one seems to have much to offer these people except the possibility of remarriage—and the divorce rate for remarriages is consistently higher than the rate for first marriages.

The literature in the area of marriage and the family is based primarily on the assumption that our institutions are healthy and that problems which arise are due to our own deficiencies. The themes are directed to adjusting *unhealthy* individuals to *healthy* institutions. However, it is our *unhealthy* institutions that have produced *unhealthy* individuals. In order to produce healthy people, institutions must be designed specifically to fulfill our basic human needs. Unlike other books, this book offers an *alternative* family structure for middle-class people who have found the traditional nuclear family and monogamous marriage somewhat inadequate in satisfying their needs. Experimentation with alternative institutions that maximize satisfaction is, perhaps, the best approach to relieving our misery and deprivation.

Beyond Marriage and the Nuclear Family is addressed to people who are looking for an alternative kind of family, a family which will emphasize true giving and sharing and which will be built around cooperation, concern, and mutual respect rather than competition, compromise, and the struggle for power and control. It is addressed to those who want the kind of family environment which gives them the greatest amount of freedom to express themselves with the least amount of restriction and coercion, but which provides them with sufficient economic and emotional security.

This book will be of great interest to those who have unsuccessfully tried to cope with feelings of emotional and economic overdependence, fear of rejection, and the inability to communicate real and suppressed feelings to their mates. It will interest individuals who have found that changing mates every few years, every few months, or even every few days does not satisfy their need for lasting intimate involvements. It will also appeal to those who find that even an *open marriage* fails to provide enough freedom for becoming a more autonomous and actualizing person.

More specifically, it will appeal to divorced parents who would like some kind of family life for themselves and their children. It also has something to offer children who are emotionally distressed as a result of being shifted from one temporary home to another as their fathers move from job to job or as their divorced parents move from mate to mate.

Beyond Marriage will also have great appeal to the elderly who end up victims of their own nuclear family. The book speaks to their feelings of uselessness, imposition, and loneliness. It suggests that their purpose in living be restored by giving them back their share of responsibility in the raising of children and by providing continuous companionship for the rest of their lives. It has appeal for the young single person as well. In the model for a new family, they would be able to select their own parents, brothers, sisters, friends, and mates, unrestricted by kinship or marital obligations.

This book is furthermore addressed to individuals who are searching for a life style which would provide them with complete privacy but also give them easy access to people who care about them and who could provide them with emotional support. The *communal family* would be a more flexible, versatile, and loosely structured unit. Paradoxically, it is the flexibility, allowing for alternative individual actions, that contributes to continuity, permanence, stability, and security.

This book has economic as well as emotional appeal. It will be of interest to individuals who would rather share some material possessions with others in order to realize and enjoy a higher standard of living than they would be able to enjoy alone. It will appeal to those who believe that cooperation with others is both economically and emotionally more satisfying than isolated individual effort and achievement.

Beyond Marriage is a book for both men and women, for people of all ages, and especially for those who believe in human equality. It presents an alternative for reasonable, open-minded, and adventurous people who are willing to experiment with new family forms that are potentially very satisfying. It is hoped that the models presented will aid in developing such family forms which will significantly reduce insecurity, jealousy, possessiveness, and competition for mates, and will increase love, intimacy, and the gratification of many other needs. The acceptance of multiple mating and multiple parentage, the abolition of kinship ties, the reevaluation of incest, the elimination of marriage, the deterministic basis of behavior, and the equal status of children and adults in the decision-making process—all are viewed as part of future families.

Deliberately designing humanistic institutions is truly one means by which we can approach our human potential. It is to our benefit to consider new alternatives. This book offers but one of these. More will surely follow as the desirability of marriage and the nuclear family decline.

The book is divided into two parts. Part One, entitled "Toward a Family of the Future," will interest both the layman and the student. It offers a critique of prevailing forms, elaborates some alternative models for interpersonal involvement, and outlines what the family might look like in the future.

Part Two, entitled "New Models in Family Theory," is designed for the person who may have more of a philosophical and theoretical interest in interpersonal relations and the emerging new morality.

The Epilogue offers a defense of the use of science and humanism in examining and experimenting with new forms of interpersonal relations and families.

Acknowledgments

I would like to express my gratitude to a number of people. For reviewing the manuscript and offering valuable criticisms, I would like to thank Jacqueline P. Wiseman (University of California, San Diego), Roger Libby (Syracuse University), Michael Gordon (University of Connecticut), Margaret Perkins (St. Petersburg Junior College), Jane Wagner (Eastfield College), Henry Olzak, and Cynthia Gliner. I am grateful to Howard Boyer, whose faith in this book has made it a reality, and to Judy Gandy, who did the copyediting. On the more personal side, I would like to thank my mother and father who reared me in an environment of acceptance, patience, and love and who tolerated my irreverent thinking and egocentric behavior. To Kris Larsen and Vicki White who had the misfortune to be married to me but the foresight to obtain a divorce, I am indeed grateful.

To my old friends and their poignant criticisms, encouragement, companionship, and emotional support, I am greatly indebted. They include Dave Brouse, Deborah Burke, Cynthia Chamberlain, Betty Collins, Philip Haysmer, John Manion, Esther Newman, James Parker, Sara Parrott, Ted Parrott, James Pennell, Betty Taylor, and Norman Waterbury. To my new friends who have had the wisdom and concern to give me reinforcement when I made sense and ignore me when I didn't, I also am indebted. They are Leslie Cameron, Sharon Duty, Robert Gliner, Susan Grumich, Linda Hickey, Charles Moran, James Reed, Lynn Versaw, and Leila Whitcombe. I have a special thanks for—Robin Anderson, Jonee Grassi, Richard Greenwood, and Ellen Speare—my new family whom I have come to love as we have developed and shared communal life. Finally, I want to acknowledge all the students who have disagreed with me and have stimulated the many changes in my ideas.

PART ONE

TOWARD A FAMILY OF THE FUTURE

The first part of the book offers a critical evaluation of the different types of interpersonal relations and family structures. Chapter 1 reviews the evidence supporting the ineffectiveness of monogamous marriage. In Chapters 2 and 3, the nuclear family's failure to satisfy our needs and its gradual decline in the light of modernization are examined. Chapter 4 discusses both actual and fictional alternative life styles. In Chapter 5, after a review of past and present family structures, a new perspective on interpersonal involvement is developed which is based upon personal commitment and dependency. This chapter is perhaps the most important because it provides the theoretical basis for much of the remaining text. The propositions in this chapter are then used, in Chapter 6, to develop four basic models. In Chapter 7, the shift from the traditional extended family to the nuclear form is traced, and the characteristics of the family of the future are projected.

1 COMMITTING MATRIMONY

> Individuals are not to be blamed for the failure of marriage: it is . . . the institution itself, perverted as it has been from the start . . . .
>
> —Simone de Beauvoir, *The Second Sex*

Why do we continue to treat the institution of marriage with reverence rather than reason? By failing to consider the possibility that other forms of coexistence might function as well in gratifying human needs, we have assumed its infallibility.

Other institutions have evolved radically in recent decades to meet the vast changes produced by technological development, urbanization, and the dramatic advances in transportation and communication. Our marriage institution, however, has remained rather static. Its assumptions and expectations have endured, but in practice we conform less and less. We feel the strain, and many of us are turning to arrangements which are not sanctioned by either the institution or society at large. Our behavior is then considered deviant, abnormal, or unhealthy. This assertion is consistent with the notion that the individual is to blame for an inability to "fit in." But this conclusion is questionable.

We turn to deviant behavior when the normally prescribed patterns of action or institutions have failed to provide for the

3

satisfaction of our needs. This is what is happening to people in the middle-class monogamous marriage predicament. Needs for prolonged intimate association are not met and free expression of affection is curtailed. Mervyn Cadwallader, a noted critic of the marriage institution, candidly describes the situation this way:

> The truth as I see it is that contemporary marriage is a wretched institution. More often than not it turns out to be a personal calamity for the happy couple. It turns out to be a mutual suicide pact disguised as a mutual improvement association. It spells the end of voluntary affection, of love freely given and joyously received. The relationship becomes constricting, coercive, and contractual.[1]

NO ALTERNATIVES

If the prevailing institution of modern marriage is as ineffective as I suggest, why is its popularity on the increase? National statistics indicate that over the past three decades the proportion of married people in the United States has gradually risen. In 1900, 59.9 percent of the male population and 58.7 percent of the female population were married as compared with 71.0 percent and 68.3 percent in 1963. Between 1960 and 1971 there has been a 13 percent increase in the number of married couples.[2]

The answer to why we continue to get married is primarily that we don't have a better alternative. In fact, we have *no* viable alternative, in spite of the feeble attempts to liberalize marital restrictions. Either we marry or we live alone. Assuming that we don't want to spend our lives in isolation, the only widespread arrangement for collective living and sexual-emotional gratification is some kind of marriage.

What options do those of us who are not married have to gratify our sexual needs? The choices seem to be masturbation, prostitution, some form of free love, or having sexual relationships outside the marriage situation. In any case, these forms of gratification are not generally condoned by society. So for regular sexual satisfaction, most people find some variety of marriage the only answer. No wonder; it's the only acceptable alternative! This problem is compounded by the mass media, who have exploited sexuality by sexualizing consumption. This titillation and enticement of sexual fantasies may in part contribute to the rise of teenage marriage and divorce rates. The emphasis on sex appeal and intense physical expression of love makes it difficult for the teenager—as well as the rest of us—to handle sexual arousals. Thus, marriage becomes a way to legitimize sex play and reduce guilt. Regular sexual gratification is not the only inducement to marry. Among other conditions leading people into early marriage are glorified images of married life, an unhappy home or the dullness of school, the ease with which young people can acquire material goods, use birth control which permits avoidance of immediate burdens of parenthood, and cultural and social patterns which encourage relationships between only two people.

With these and other inducements, young people, as well as older persons who are single, divorced, or widowed, are led to believe that marriage is the only answer to personal problems. But marriage does not solve these problems, even with more open marital relationships becoming acceptable. The rising divorce rates attest to this. The primary reason single people of all kinds get married is because marriage, however interpreted, is our only alternative. If we assume that the institution of marriage is not functioning because it fails to gratify certain needs and that it is the only institution available for such gratification, then our choice is either to fit in and adjust to an ineffective structure or to remain single. Our choice is to get married and be frustrated or to stay single and be insecure.

MARRIAGE ASKS TOO MUCH

Within the institution of marriage, we expect total and permanent involvement between two people. We want our marriage partner to satisfy any needs whenever and as long as we need gratification. This is too much to ask of any person. Realistically, it is impossible. In her discussion of "The Married Woman," Simone de Beauvoir argues that when a man and a woman are obligated to satisfy each other in every way throughout their lives, a monstrosity is produced that gives rise to hypocrisy, lying, hostility, and unhappiness.[3] When we become that dependent upon one another for a long period of time, the fears of rejection and of losing our partner as the sole source of gratification tends to produce a situation in which possessiveness and jealousy thrive. To avoid treating loved ones as property we might establish less than total involvements. That is, we might develop relationships with other people so that when one person cannot satisfy a given need, we can turn to alternative sources. This of course is alien to monogamous marriage. So, we have another dilemma: choosing between marriage which can lead us to overdependence, possessiveness, and exclusive gratification; and staying single which can lead us to isolation, insecurity, superficial involvement, and undergratification.

MARRIAGE DESTROYS ROMANTIC LOVE

Romantic love in our culture is supposed to be the foundation of marriage. In its present form, however, it seems quite contrary to what married life is all about. The discrepancy between the ideal notion of love and the reality of married existence produces in many cases disillusionment, turmoil, and divorce. Albert Ellis, a leading sexologist, argues that

> marriage . . . invariably means domesticity: meaning, a constant, more or less monotonous, living together on an hour after hour, year after year basis. Indeed, if romantic lovers wanted, with perfect logic, to induce their passions to endure for a maximum period of time, they might well ban, almost under any circumstances, marital domesticity.[4]

He further maintains that romantic love particularly thrives on intermittent rather than steady association between two lovers. This follows the research of behaviorists (such as Skinner) who find that mild positive reinforcement at variable intervals is most effective in conditioning our responses. If this kind of patterning is most conducive to prolongation of love, then perhaps our institutions should be structured so that lovers interact at intermittent rather than regular intervals. Ellis illustrates this proposition by commenting that individuals who are raised to crave romantic love are rarely content with anything but the sustained emotional intensity which is not common to everyday marital life. He argues that romantic love as the exclusive basis of marriage is hopelessly inadequate. Perhaps he should have argued that marriage as an institution is hopelessly inadequate for the prolongation of romantic love and its intense emotional demands. After all, he does suggest some positive and appealing implications of romantic relationships, including democracy of choice, freedom from restraint, aspirations to high-level individualism, and glorious potentialities for human ecstasy.

Although romantic love has its advantages, in its origin it was quite opposed to erotic love. Romantic love in essence was pursuit without fulfillment, and thus there was little chance of developing deep and meaningful relationships. My contention here is not that romantic love is ideal, only that some of its more positive qualities are destroyed in monogamous marriage situations. The kind of romantic love I refer to here is most characteristic of premarital relationships of dating and courtship. The love which evolves in marriage is somewhat different; it becomes a more dependent, possessive, and jealous love.

Well, this all may sound quite reasonable, but does happiness really decrease as a result of being married? In their popular text, *The Adjusted American*, Snell and Gail Putney characterize romantic love as a projection of qualities which we would like to experience in ourselves but do not. We then project these qualities onto our mates, where we adore them.

He then begins to act as if this person were an extension of himself. Longing to enjoy the misplaced part of himself, he clings to the person on whom he has projected it, he is possessive and jealous, he delights in the loved one's presence, but feels anxious and incomplete when the person is absent.[5]

After several years of marriage and constant association, however, the nature of the relationship changes. Idealized images fade, and negative projections appear. Additional evidence confirmed that the increase in length of marriage is associated with an increase in unfavorable perceptions of the spouse. These findings showed that the longer couples were married, the more likely they were to see their spouse as not well-thought-of by others, and to perceive less gratefulness, appreciation, and willingness to accept advice on the part of the spouse. In effect, the longer the couples were married, the less favorable personality qualities each member saw in the other.[6]

If this evidence is valid—that the less time we are married the happier we tend to be—it makes sense to postulate that love and happiness can be maximized if marriage is shortened or abolished altogether. Short of this extreme position, is it at all possible or feasible to create an institution which at least stabilizes love and happiness? It almost seems too much to ask for a new institution which enhances love and happiness. At the present time our choice appears to be to stay married for short periods of time and be happy and loving or stay married for long periods of time and be relatively unhappy and unloving.

De Beauvoir summarizes the inherent conflict between marital obligations and their negative effects on the spontaneity of loving. She charges that

> marriage is obscene in principle in so far as it transforms into rights and duties those mutual relations which should be founded on a spontaneous urge; it gives an instrumental and therefore degrading character to the two bodies in dooming them to know each other in their general aspects *as* bodies, not as persons.[7]

MARRIAGE CONFINES LOVE

Marriage not only destroys love but commonly limits it to our own mate and our own children. To increase the durability of a marriage, we must decrease the attractiveness of alternative relationships. When spouses have attractions outside of marriage, possibilities of divorce seem to increase. In his review of the literature in this area, George Levinger concludes that anywhere from 15 to 35 percent of all cases of divorce action have been due to preferences for outside sexual partners.[8]

Monogamy obviously does not condone the extension of erotic love to second and third parties. Whether or not this is morally right or wrong is not the question here. Marriage does in fact curtail this kind of love. The prevailing myth is that we cannot romantically love more than one person. It seems strangely inconsistent that we can love more than one child or more than one friend or more than one parent, but that erotic love becomes exclusive, restrictive, and limited by moral and legal dictate.

Not only does marriage confine erotic love to one person, it also tends not to work as well when there is too much of an attachment to our friends or even our kin. It was reported that competing close group affiliations are associated with divorce proneness. What this amounts to is that the weaker the identifications with other groups, the stronger the marriage bond. But is it desirable to weaken outgroup loyalty? Research has also shown that the stronger the ingroup loyalty, the stronger the outgroup hostility. The least disrupted marriages are those in which the couple live some distance from the two kin networks and manifest little emotional dependence upon kin.[9] If successful marriage is dependent upon ingroup loyalty and cohesiveness, it would seem to follow that successful marriage is associated with some increased hostility toward outgroups, whether they be friends, relatives, or lovers. Relative isolation of the married couple from competing groups then seems to be a precondition for successful marriages. Whether or not the evidence supports this logic remains to be seen.

Monogamy idealizes the cohesiveness of the couple. On the other hand, not getting married implies some isolation and in many situations, extreme loneliness. Yet extreme loneliness cannot be cured by marriage. Perhaps loneliness is more tolerable by those who live alone. They have no expectations and thus no disappointments. But should loneliness and isolation be tolerated by either the married or the single? We are faced again with a dilemma. Our choice is to get married and be isolated and lonely or to stay single and be isolated and lonely. It is not social stigma but the relative social isolation which is the bane of the unmarried. What really seems to be the case is that isolation is also the bane of the married—especially the married woman.

> In the early years of marriage the wife often lulls herself with illusions . . . then her true sentiments become clear; she sees that her husband could get along very well without her, that her children are bound to get away from her and to be always more or less ungrateful. The home no longer saves her from empty liberty; she finds herself alone, forlorn, a subject; and she finds nothing to do with herself. Affectionate attachments and habitual ways may still be a great help, but not a salvation. All sincere women writers have noted the melancholy in the heart of "the woman of thirty;" . . . They sing gaily at the beginning of married life and maternity, but later on they manifest a certain distress. It is a remarkable fact that in France [the home of the authoress] suicide is less common in married than in unmarried women up to age thirty, but not thereafter.[10]

Although a few studies have shown that the suicide rate for single people is higher than for married people, this trend might reverse itself as new organizations and institutions are developed for single people and as single people begin to feel that they can live a productive and fulfilling life outside of the marriage go-round. As reported in a recent study, the hypothesis that married people have lower suicide rates than single people was rejected.[11] The male's loneliness, although tempered by job associations and perhaps occasional adulterous relations, is somewhat moderated. Because of his total commitment at home, his outside involvements seem doomed to superficiality.

Some extramarital involvement is commonly permitted within the institutional framework. Flirtation in traditional groups, for example, typically is limited to mixing bridge and dancing partners. More liberal norms in some groups involve more physical contact. Practices ranging from tolerated sexual caresses away from the group to open wife-trading are becoming more common. The apparent need of married people to engage in these different practices again illustrates a failure of the institution in providing full satisfaction of social emotional requirements.

Some very provocative cross-cultural research has been conducted suggesting strong relationships between the violent nature of societies and the extent to which they restrict physical affection. James Prescott and Cathy McKay found that societies most characterized by "murdering, killing, and torturing of their enemies" are also characterized by depriving infants of physical affection, and punishing premarital and extramarital sexual behavior. If there is a society that is permissive in terms of allowing both premarital and extramarital sexual behavior, the chances of that society being a violent one are less than one in a thousand. If adult violence is undesirable, the above findings, according to the authors, raise some serious questions about the values of virginity, chastity, and monogamous sexual relationships in human societies.[12]

In review, then, marriage both destroys and confines love. But what are the alternatives to the present structure which might promote and extend it? Ellis suggests the following revisions for prolonging romantic attachments:

> Romantic love may . . . be sustained by severely limiting the period of its expression.

> Romantic love may flower indefinitely if lovers consciously become varietists and change their individual partners while continuing their romantic patterns of attachment.

Romantic lovers may, quite logically: engage in plural love affairs and thus, by having two or more romantic partners simultaneously, avoid much of the monotony and domesticity which normally dooms romanticism.[13]

In terms of marriage, this would quickly destroy possessive and restrictive monogamy. Such a pluralistic structure would require drastic modifications in the present-day forms of marriage and family. Pluralism in this sense, moreover, is being practiced, and practiced more and more openly. If this is the trend, we should consider the possibility of incorporating these new norms into the institutional framework rather than continuing to pretend that they do not exist, do not satisfy our needs, and do not bring about more interpersonal fulfillment.

MARRIAGE IS UNDEMOCRATIC

Marriage as the basis for the nuclear family perpetuates the glorification of kinship ties. Although these ties are weaker than they were in the traditional family, they persist. Our relationships are worthwhile because they are with relatives, not friends. Responsibility and care are prescribed in our kinship system. Offspring, as the human product of marriage, are first in line to inherit the rewards of the elders. Whom children select as mates is thus of supreme importance to parents, for it is *their* wealth and *their* care which are at stake. Because elders have traditionally controlled the rewards (especially economic ones), they have demanded control in the selection of mates for their children. This arrangement often can be coercive and threatening. In a traditional family structure, it can hardly be treated lightly.

The control of mate selection by the older generation is especially important when large inheritances are in question. Kinship ties are perhaps the best predictor of the wealth of younger members of society. There seems to be a strong relationship between the social class standing of parents and that of their offspring. The continuation of the traditional marriage and family pattern thus is obviously in the interest of the more conservative upper classes.

But if this undemocratic control of the young by the old and wealthy is undesirable, kinship relationships will have to be reconsidered. Mate selection, in order to be open and unrestricted, necessitates a loosening of kinship ties.[14]

If it is preferable to have more democratic structures such as equal economic opportunities for all children, not just the children of the rich inheriting the riches, then, among other changes, the traditional kinship lines must be broken. Our choice is to maintain the traditional kinship ties which perpetuate inheritance, social class differences, and family loyalty, or to destroy the emphasis on kinship patterns and begin to bring about a more egalitarian family and social system.

If this sort of breakdown in family lineage is possible, we must create other means of defining the boundaries of the family. Perhaps friendship relationships would serve in this function. There is some indication that most people have strong and multiple memberships in other groups which could meet many of the needs supplied by the traditional kin network.[15] Is it reasonable to assume that people are closer emotionally when the cohesive factor is based upon friendship rather than kinship? Is a family of friends better able to meet the needs of its members than a family of relatives? We will pursue these questions in detail as we progress in the text. Chapter 7 summarizes the characteristics of a new kind of family based upon democratic decision making and friendship ties.

2 THE FRAGMENTED FAMILY

> The family may neither vanish nor enter upon a new
> Golden Age. It may—and this is far more
> likely—break up, shatter, only to come together
> again in weird and novel ways.
>
> —Alvin Toffler, *Future Shock*

Compared with our modern nuclear family, our traditional extended family was generally more supportive. The early American family, for example, was dominated and controlled by the father, and women were expected, primarily for economic reasons, to have several children. The early family as a group was composed of husband and wife, numerous children, children's children, and dependent relatives. Spinsters and widows were in great demand for their competence in household management, and adult male relatives were assets because of their ability to work the land and contribute to the family income. Many families, usually related, lived close to one another and shared the responsibilities for providing economic and psychological aid to other family members. Children typically had several adults of each sex with whom they could closely identify.

As the children developed strong emotional ties to relatives other than their biological parents, their dependencies for economic as well as psychological rewards became more dispersed. Because of this diffused involvement, children in the early American family could tap several sources of gratification. In the event that one or both of their parents left the family setting, were deceased, or even temporarily rejected them, the children had easy access to other adults who were willing to care for them and assume the roles of their parents. Because of the larger size of the family clan, a great deal of security for the children was built into the structure itself.

Although this kind of family provided for economic and psychological security in the rearing of children, in other respects it was quite restrictive. Occupational choices were extremely limited, roles were rigidly defined, and strong punishments were handed out to those who dared to innovate. Social mobility, both up and down in the class structure and from one position to another at the same social level, was curtailed in the former by an inflexible caste or status structure and in the latter by custom and tradition. Membership in a family was usually determined along blood lines and by marriages planned and controlled by family elders.

The authoritarian traditional family was usually headed by a strong patriarch. There was little respect for women and children who were relegated to lower status positions. The presence of a rigid hierarchy of family positions with privileged persons filling the top ranks was apparent in most traditional societies. An excessive demand on conformity, order, and obedience was reflected in the symbolism and the seriousness of the family rituals. Many people seemed to be property or possessions of someone else (for example, slaves, concubines, child labor, subservient wives) and people functioned according to highly restrictive roles and values. There was little or no opportunity for rebellion or change.

Our traditional family, then, had some characteristics which contributed to increasing need-satisfaction and some which did not. The extended structure provided the opportunity for children as well as adults to develop a larger number of deep and more meaningful relationships within the family itself. This could have led to a greater amount of economic and psychological security if it weren't for the many accompanying restrictions, taboos, and authoritarian impositions. There was little question of the identity of each member, for few if any alternatives were available and expected behavior was rigidly constructed. These limitations, because they were largely pre-determined, failed to take individual differences into account. Individuals, for example, could not select their own mates nor the number of mates. They could not easily move from one community to another without greatly disrupting the course of family living. Rather than encouraging people to go into positions which corresponded to their own traits, capacities, and interests, these capacities and interests were made to fit roles dictated by age, sex, and social class of parents.

THE NUCLEAR FAMILY

Frustrations and discontent arising from the failure of our traditional family to adapt to individual needs laid the groundwork for its eventual breakdown. In addition, the Industrial Revolution, bringing the deterioration of an agrarian economy, gave impetus to a growing technology. Because of better forms of communication and transportation, family and individual mobility became more prominent and acceptable. The migration from a small, highly personal, and integrated family situation to a more impersonal, bureaucratic, and urban environment had the effect of fragmenting the relatively stable and secure extended structure.

Two conclusions can be drawn from examining these changes in family structure.

1. Children and adults in the *traditional structure* had a greater amount of psychological security due to the larger number of people who served as dependable sources of emotional and affective gratification, but they had a great deal of

frustration due to the rigid system's failure to allow for the expression of individual differences.

2. Children and adults in the *nuclear structure* have much less psychological security and fewer emotional resources, due to the small size of the unit, but have increased mobility, flexibility, and freedom to make choices, due to increased structuring for individual differences.

Our nuclear family evolved favorably in all respects except in the area of providing increased security and emotional benefits for its members. Although the fragmentation of the extended form, because of its psychologically threatening implications, should be considered an undesirable trend, the breakdown of traditional authoritarian structures which occurs in the nuclear type can be seen as a more positive development.

> One could, for example, point to many liberating effects which this change has brought about. It has liberated creative activities from the bondage of familistic servitude and opened up the personality market for freer unfolding of talent, aptitude, and individualistic choice. In short, one must not lose sight of the general principle that any change brings about a host of reactions. Some may be judged functional and some dysfunctional.[1]

Today, the traditional extended family structure and norms have almost completely disappeared. Our primary socializing agency, the extended family, failed to adapt to a modern growing industrialized world. From the shattered extended family, a residual, smaller, and more mobile nuclear structure emerged. The general characteristics of this newer family contrast sharply with the traditional type. Blood relatives are located throughout a wider geographic area and children must rely more upon parents than other relatives for economic and psychological support. These conditions as well as the smaller size of the unit and the detached and depersonalized surroundings of urban life, result in a lesser sense of family security.

In other respects, the nuclear family offers us an increasing amount of flexibility, mobility, and emancipation from the traditional family's rigid and discriminatory practices. Choice of occupation is a function of interest and capacities, rather than being ascribed. Because of the breakdown of the rigid caste system, the possibility of upward social mobility increases, allowing for greater variation in the selection of roles. Younger members of the traditional family migrate to larger urban centers, breaking down the authority of the family elders and providing themselves with the opportunity to select their own mates and govern their own family units. A more recent trend emancipating women from narrow household and child-rearing duties, as well as from male domination, allows them wider choices in deciding occupation and general life style. The relaxing of the traditional structure thus enables family members who were most discriminated against to rebel and to search for new identities.

However, alternative institutions which center around more egalitarian values are not readily available. Because of this, an increasing number of single and divorced people who are in some way involved in a personal crisis are desperately searching for a new way of life but have no place to go, no institution to identify with, and no hope of enjoying any kind of family living. Their alienation and despair suggests the grave necessity for experimenting with and institutionalizing new life styles and family forms. Some of these alternatives are reviewed in Chapter 4.

SIZE OF THE FAMILY

One of the major changes that has been taking place in our family is the gradual decrease in the number of members constituting a unit. The average size of the U.S. household decreased from 5.5 per unit in 1850 to 3.14 in 1971.[2] As a result of this decrease, our family seems to be moving toward more and more isolation residentially and economically; with this fragmentation it is becoming less able to meet the more generalized traditional functions. The family now focuses on socialization and the exchange of emotional support and affection. The small size of our nuclear family and its isolation thus have ramifications on the socialization process of children and their emotional security. Parent-child tensions are increased, leading to a greater possibility of dissolution. As the family unit becomes smaller, the chances for parental error increase. "Each child becomes more crucial."[3]

Somewhat contrary to these notions are findings suggesting that smaller families are less authoritarian, and that there is more parental affection toward children and vice versa and thus less parental stress.[4] Perhaps the crucial factor is the ratio of children to parent figures in the family unit. Maybe larger families with larger numbers of adults than children will show the most favorable dispositions and gratifications on the part of the members. Such a family might be more representative of the general population in terms of age distribution. If there are about two or three adults for each child in society, perhaps this ratio could be maintained in larger families not based upon kinship. Our children would have several parental models to relate to in contrast to the situation in large middle-class families where many children in the unit are confined to one or two parent relationships. Tension and competition for affection could be lessened allowing for greater integration in the family.

Parents also use children to satisfy their own needs, sometimes more than they use themselves to satisfy the children's needs. They "hang on" their children their own unrealized potential and see not the child but the projected image of the person they themselves would like to be. The loving parents clothe their children with a great deal of themselves and cling to the children possessively. The fewer the number of children they have, the more intense the desire to retain their property. In a more extended family or in the family with a larger number of children, this need on the part of the parents to possess their children might be decreased or at least diffused.

Because of the possessive demands which many of us impose upon our children, there is an increased tension which occurs in the life cycle of the family as the children reach maturity and begin to break the parental ties. This tension is aggravated by the extreme dependence on the parents encouraged in the small nuclear family. The lack of continuity, as family members grow up and move into adult roles, is a weakness in the nuclear structure. The move involves breaking off old ties and creating a new family unit which is stable largely to the extent to which the new marriage is stable. The probability of this stability resulting is rather dismal as seen later in a review of the trends in divorce rates.

Children's emotional identification and dependency upon one adult male and one adult female are also limiting factors in our modern family. In our extended family, young boys and girls could choose models from among a number of visible adult relatives and could derive an image of what he or she wanted to be. But in the nuclear family such choice is limited, particularly if one parent is not easily observable. As a consequence, children of nuclear families seek models in their peer groups and adults outside of the family setting. Generally, these models lead to conflicts in loyalties, value systems, and time commitments.

I previously suggested that parents should have more than one child, so as to decentralize their possessiveness and dependency upon any one of them. Perhaps children should have more than one parent of each sex, so as to provide them with a larger number of consistent, available, and dependable role models. I am acquainted, for example, with an experimental extended family consisting of three adult males, three adult females, and two children. They have been together for several years, have pooled their resources, and have shared child-rearing responsibilities. When one of the father figures is not available, the children gain in the security that they can turn to one or both of the other adult males in the family. When one of the "mothers" is not particularly interested in the kind of activity desired by the children, the children can find an adult female more receptive to their needs. Each of the children has three adults of each sex to provide them with multiple role models and increased options in obtaining the kinds of gratifications that parents provide. The children seem to be quite content with their family life. Having more than two parents thus stabilizes socialization and allows for better solutions to problems related to family crisis.

If these criticisms of the size of the modern nuclear form are valid, perhaps we should reconsider some variation of an extended family model. This might be even more important when we are reminded that children of the divorced, because they generally only have one adult to identify with at any given time, suffer without the more generalized emotional support that was so common in traditional extended clans. With the development of working mothers and baby-sitting, security is absurdly minimized in that our children are subjected to an environment which provides for the least amount of genuine care and the maximum amount of superficial and temporary involvement.

SEX-ROLE DIFFERENCES

It is an understatement that the role of the adult male in the marriage and family institutions has been traditionally different from that of the adult female. Men were socially independent, complete individuals. Women, confined to reproductive and domestic roles, were never considered equal to men, those producers whose existence was justified by the work they did. The expectations of the husband-father in the nuclear structure are still highly differentiated from those of the wife-mother.

It is my contention that these role differences and inequalities contribute significantly to the breakdown of the modern family. In discussing this, I will not be concerned with the fact women are biologically and physiologically different from men, only that sex-role differences are systematically produced primarily through child-rearing practices. These practices are defined by the norms of society in general and by the role structure of the nuclear family in particular. The role definitions and the norms which support them will be the target for discussion. I will direct my remarks and evidence to the personality and behavioral effects of the roles in the nuclear family.

Self-Alienation

Expectations in the family generally require, among other things, that men be more rational, independent, aggressive, self-confident, innovative, realistic, and competitive than women. Women are expected to be more emotional, dependent, passive, self-conscious, conventional, idealistic, and compassionate than men. By not allowing each sex to display the characteristics attributed to the opposite sex, half of these personality traits are suppressed. Males, for example, may feel inadequate if they fail to control their emotions, become dependent upon females in some way, or are not interested in competitive activities. Females, on the other hand, may feel some negative social pressures if they become too intellectual, respond aggressively, or become economically independent. Thus, each sex must hold back half of its potentials so as to fit into the prevailing structure.

My concern is what happens to us when this sort of structure is imposed upon us. The Putneys' thesis concerning the "adjusted American" is again relevant. They suggest that those traits which are ascribed to the other sex are alienated from ourselves. Because we cannot accept these traits in ourselves (cannot admit that we have these potentials), we project them onto members of the other sex.

> Having alienated those aspects of himself which he has learned to regard as incompatible with his manhood, the male projects them onto the women around him. In his mother, his daughter, his wife, and particularly his sweetheart, he sees and loves his own desire to be dependent, vain, impractical, demonstrative, and all the other things he has learned to consider unsuitable in

himself. Indeed, he often demands that his women display such characteristics.

In a parallel but reverse manner, the little girl in America is encouraged to seek comfort when she scrapes a knee, to be openly affectionate, to be proud of her curls and ruffles—and is scolded for a dirty face or a bold manner. She learns to alienate her potential for being aggressive, self-assertive, proficient in sports and mechanics. She is likely to adore masterful men.[5]

As we project these alienated aspects of ourselves onto our mates, however, we also desire to reunite with them. When the projections become very strong, we become miserable without their constant presence. We are jealous of anyone else who is close to our spouse, for we want exclusive and constant possession of the potential we project.[6]

Sex-role differences thus restrict us from expressing half of our humanity. The sex-role structure in the family is ineffective in that it leads to self-alienation, projection, restrictions in expressing certain behaviors and emotions, mate idealizations, possessiveness, and jealousy.

Cross-Sex Empathy

Because males and females have been socialized into such different kinds of roles, they have become different kinds of people with different kinds of behaviors, attitudes, and feelings. A common complaint among husbands and wives is that their spouses do not understand them. This might be attributed to the differences in the way they were raised. These differences make it more difficult for them to put themselves symbolically in the place of their mates and to feel and think as their mates feel and think. If being able to empathize with one's spouse is an important part of understanding, and understanding and empathy between men and women are desirable, then perhaps the perpetuation of differences in the roles of males and females in the modern family should be halted.

Intimacy

Intimacy to some extent emerges with empathy and understanding. These qualities seem less apparent when couples are products of different role prescriptions. I would also expect that as two people become more intimate, their antagonisms would tend to be reduced. George Bach maintains in *The Intimate Enemy* that when partners don't fight they are not involved in an intimate relationship.[7] However, when hostility arises between partners, the blame should more properly be attributed to marital expectations. The institution places its demands and restrictions on the couple, producing aggressive and hostile feelings. These feelings are not inevitable, but are socially determined. The practice, which Bach advocates, of learning to "fight fair" in marriage is a poor substitute for discovering new forms which will bring aggression from inevitability to extinction. I agree that aggression and frustration are inevitable, given the prevailing marriage institution, but not inevitable or even common in other social contexts. Bach is obviously treating the hostile effects of marriage, not the causes. To make an analogy: cancer is an inevitable disease; let's live with it through radiation treatments rather than find its causes. Given marriage, I suppose we need the treatments, but let's not assume that we have to put up with a major cause of hostility—marriage itself.

In a study of male-female interaction, it was found that with more intimacy, the dominant sex in each pair became less dominant. Thus, there was a decline in traditional sex-role differences with increased intimacy.[8] If we are interested in bringing about more intimacy among people, then this result suggests that a de-emphasis of sex-role distinctions might be a move in the desired direction.

Sex-role differences are imposed upon us rather early in life. During adolescence the norms in dating groups emphasize sexual antagonism and exploitation, since males and females gain prestige in peer groups in directly opposite ways: the male by maximizing physical contact and minimizing expenses, the female by minimizing the former and maximizing the latter. Intimacy is minimized if each partner, even during physical contact, is keeping an account with regard to these dating norms.

These opposing norms then create social distance between males and females at an early age, and it is no surprise that this distance, antagonism, and exploitation later carry over into the family setting. Thus, the nuclear family is not functioning to the extent to which it curtails an early, more open and frank interchange between the sexes leading to the development of intimacy. Sex-role distinctions learned by the young do not contribute to that end.

Sexuality and Sex-Roles

If sex-role differences lead to antagonism and a lack of intimacy, it would seem to follow that in situations in which these differences are magnified, problems in heterosexuality would be more common. In a cross-cultural study of marital sexuality, Lee Rainwater concluded that in societies with separation in the roles of husbands and wives, the couple will not develop a close sexual relationship, and the wife will not find sexual relations with her husband sexually gratifying.[9] Although the evidence is limited, sex-role distinctions seem to detract from satisfying sexual relationships.

Personality Correlates

What kinds of personalities do people who believe in the virtues of maintaining role distinctions between the sexes have? In a recent study of 284 college sophomores, I found that those subjects who favored the traditional roles of males and females also tended to be significantly

1. More racially prejudiced.
2. More authoritarian.
3. More schizophrenic.

4. More dogmatic.
5. More marriage oriented.
6. Less self-autonomous.
7. Less self-esteemed.

It is interesting to note that they also tended to agree that "familiarity breeds contempt."[10] These finding seem to confirm some of the previous discussion and research reports.

In summary, it is my contention that the sex-role structure in the modern family is unfavorable in that it promotes prejudicial, dogmatic, and authoritarian attitudes; it promotes self-alienation, projection, and a lack of self-esteem and autonomy; it blocks effective communication, understanding, and intimacy; it destroys cross-sex empathy; it magnifies social distance, antagonism, and exploitation between the sexes; and it leads to dissatisfaction in sexual relationships.

ROLE OF THE FEMALE

The problems inherent in the role of the female are of no recent origin. It is a part of the long-standing Christian tradition.

> Unto the women [God] said, I will greatly multiply thy sorrow and thy conception; in sorrow thou shalt bring forth children; and thy desire shall be to thy husband, and he shall rule over thee.
> —Genesis 3:16

And, as ruling husbands, men have imposed the duties which they found less desirable upon their wives. And their wives, as good Christian wives, have learned their roles well and have even thought these duties were honorable and fulfilling. But only when women decided to question the role structure of the "sacred" family were they able to see, in an objective sense, the inequality, the oppression, and the exploitation built into the traditional female role.

In the traditional role, women are not given the opportunity to grow to their full capacities and to retain their human individuality. They have been bought off by men to be content with washing diapers, cleaning house, buying groceries, and the like. Their reward is economic security; the cost, in many cases, is sexual and emotional gratification for their husbands. Perhaps it is not an exaggeration to call the state of the housewife a sickness. Betty Friedan asks if the house of the American suburban wife is in reality a comfortable concentration camp. She suggests that they have adjusted to their biological role and have become dependent, passive, childlike; they have given up their adult status to live at a lower human level. The work they do is simple, endless, monotonous, and unrewarding.[11]

The increasing isolation of the nuclear family is best exemplified in the housewife role, for the male is out of the house all day and therefore can be neither overlord nor companion.

> With the father absent, radio and television provide the mother with a watery substitute for adult companionship. A young colleague told me recently that his wife leaves the radio on all day merely to hear the sound of a grown-up voice. The continual chatter of little children can be profoundly irritating, even to a naturally affectionate person. The absence of servants from nearly all American middle class households brings the wife face to face with the brutalizing features of motherhood and housework. If she had the mentality of a peasant, she might be able to cope with them more easily.[12]

But this isolation, leading to emotional and intellectual poverty, is not universal. In societies in which the domestic role works, the housewife is part of a large extended family or a close-knit village community or both. Both the small size of the nuclear family and its isolated nature contribute to the restrictions imposed upon the average housewife. But what happens to her under these kinds of conditions?

Many women attempt to escape the monotony and boredom of their daily existence. Perhaps TV soap operas provide the greatest escape for the American housewife. The afternoon "soaps" foster an ideology based upon female passivity, ineptness, and subservience, even for women of the highest professional status. They are raped, divorced, abandoned, misunderstood, given drugs, attacked by mysterious diseases and go mad, and have more brain tumors and die more than the males do. The TV commercials follow the same pattern, showing women inside of the home involved in household tasks 43 percent of the time, as adjuncts to men 38 percent of the time, and 17 percent of the time as sex objects. The plots in these series may make the housewife feel safe and secure but may make these same viewers dissatisfied with their own dull lives. When she turns off the TV, looks into the mirror, and greets her husband, the comparison is not pleasant.[13] Thus, women use the mass media, the soap operas, the love magazines, and the gossip they can conjure up in coffee sessions with neighbors as mechanisms for creating fantasies. In these fantasies, they live as they would like to live, but they live vicariously, not in the real world. Their escape from reality only points out the possibility of a more severe problem: a total reliance upon fantasies for satisfying needs frustrated by the family system. The possibility of schizophrenia, or even worse, suicide, looms over them.

Others may try to recreate themselves through their children. They may project so much of themselves onto their daughter or son that they find the child's presence indispensable. The "adjusted" American mother, in this context, maintains the needs of her child leaving little time for other things. This she sees as evidence of her conscientiousness. She insists that a child needs her full attention and that she loves her baby so much she is glad to devote her life to her child. The latter is true enough. The result may well be a continuous destructive interference with the life of the child and an inevitable emptiness in her own.

If she cannot find fulfillment through her children, she may turn to material things. Since she *does* nothing, she seeks self-fulfillment in what she *has*. If these material possessions become her raison d'être, she could spend her days endlessly polishing and cleaning them, always being prepared to display them proudly to whoever might pass by. She eventually loses sight of *who she is,* for all of her rewards come as a result of *what she has.*

When fantasy, vicarious living, and materialism have failed, she still has two realistic alternatives, neither of which contributes to the maintenance of the old family. Either a job or an affair may serve as a release from domesticity.

Another problem which faces the woman in the family is her role in the completion of the child-rearing functions. Increasingly, child rearing is concentrated into a substantially shorter period of time than before. As of the most recent information, women are on the average likely to bear their last child at the age of 30 or 31. Thus, partly by living longer in a better state of health and partly by reducing the time span of their primary attention to motherhood, women are freed for other functions. There is a vacuum between the ages of 40 or 45 until death, an average of about 30 years. I already noted the increased suicide rate of women over 40. This would suggest a deterioration of their psychological well-being, to say the least. A study of Vassar graduates who were 20 or 25 years out of college showed that for the most part they were adjusted as suburban housewives, conscientious mothers, and were active in their communities. It was also found, however, that upon graduation they did not continue to grow mentally, emotionally, or personally, and after 20 years, those with the most psychological problems were the most traditionally feminine.[14]

The role of the housewife thus seems detrimental to the growth and development of middle-aged women. It defines their function as child rearing but fails to provide a meaningful alternative function once the children are reared. It is almost impossible for elderly women to participate in a child-rearing role later in life, given the present evolution of the family.

The housewife role, in summary, limits the aspirations which most women have of reaching their full potential. They are commonly exploited and forced to become parasites. In their traditional role, they fail to grow mentally, emotionally, and personally; in the more isolated family setting, they are left with fantasy, materialism, possessiveness of their children, and a feeling of emptiness in their later years. The fate of the married woman, as expressed by de Beauvoir, is one of becoming "a gilded mediocrity lacking ambition and passion, of aimless days indefinitely repeated, of living a life that slips away gently toward death without questioning its purpose."[15] The prognosis is more positive. Women's roles are beginning to become more optional and diversified. As the possibilities for new wife and mother roles increase, there might emerge a more egalitarian sex role structure in the family of the future.

ROLE OF THE MALE

The male's role in the family perhaps is more appealing than the female's. He initially marries to obtain anchorage which satisfies his sexual-emotional needs and provides him with a sense of belonging and of self-esteem. He desires to confine his wife and children to the home for ready access to his gratifications, but not to be himself confined. He is bored by repetition, and seeks novelty, opposition, risks, and friends outside the marriage unit.

But the absence of the father from the family setting in many situations places a good deal of stress on the stability of the marriage and upon the father-child relationship. The successful maintenance of the family unit is partially a function of the extent to which the father is present. When occupational and military obligations call him away for long periods of time, family continuity is disrupted. The children lose the one adult male model with whom they can identify and the wife is left without the one male companion the institution allows her. During this period, the wife has to assume some responsibility for the children that would normally belong to the husband. When the father returns, the roles must be redistributed and the lines of authority reestablished. In a research project during

World War II, Reuben Hill discovered that it was not always easy for the couple to "pick up where they left off" when the father returned from the armed forces. An unpublished study was made of blue-collar construction workers who had to work out of town. Almost all of these men agreed such jobs posed real problems for them and their families.[16]

An additional problem is that the family is not designed for a mobile father. The needs which the family supplies to the father are also commonly frustrated during his departure. He is expected to remain faithful and lonely until the time he can be reunited with his family. If his commitment to his wife is exercised, he endures his frustration. When this happens, the family system can be seen as reinforcing sexual-emotional masochism on the part of the wife as well as the husband. If the commitment is not abided by, extramarital relationships may lead to deceit at least, or at most, to dissolution of the marriage.

The stability of the family is also contingent upon the sexual compatibility of the couple. Family stress is more likely to occur if the husband is not a satisfactory lover or becomes involved with another woman. Men are expected to be faithful to their wives or leave the home and marry "the other woman." What all of this means is that if anything happens to the marriage, the male may find himself separated from his children, in spite of his honest desires to be a good father.

The closeness between the father and his children is dependent upon a close relationship between the man and his wife. Family norms place strong emotional pressures upon the father as he is torn away from his children due to an incompatible marriage. The increased mobility of the father, due to occupational or military obligations, as well as the expectation that he leave the family setting in case of an incompatible marriage, both contribute to a weakening of the father-child relationship and the loss of the only adult male model for male children. Kingsley Davis argued that the weak link in the family group is this father-child bond. He maintained that there is no necessary association and no easy means of identification between the two as between the mother and child.[17] The weak bond between father and child may be attributed to the trend which gives the father more freedom and mobility and more access to additional sexual involvements.

Our family has thus failed to evolve in a direction which would allow for this increased mobility and still provide a basis for family stability, strong bonds between adult males and children, and an adult male role model. It also fails to provide for continuous sexual-emotional gratification for separated parents whether the separation be one day or a divorce.

SEXUALITY NORMS

Our old nuclear family has a monogamous structure. The couple enact a contract wherein they explicitly agree that other intimate relationships with the same or the other sex shall cease and each partner shall be the sole source of comfort and gratification for the other. Within these norms exists an assumption that it is only possible to love one mate. We as spouses are expected to meet each of our partner's sexual and emotional demands and in effect come to accept the equation of our mate satisfying our needs with the needs themselves. So long as our spouse is ever-present to satisfy frustrated needs (which doesn't happen), there is no problem. Even if habitual behaviors are not effective, we have difficulty recognizing this fact or altering our behaviors. What I am suggesting is that norms which provide for only one source of gratification, as does monogamy, are not adequate. They provide no alternative means of sexual-emotional satisfaction. In specifying our mate as the sole means of meeting these needs, such norms prevent continuous gratification and frequently lead to neurosis.[18] Part of this neurosis can be attributed to the more or less total mutual dependency that the members of the couple develop for each other, which in turn may lead in monogamy to monotony, restrictiveness, the demise of romantic love, and other evils.

Perhaps one of these "evils" is the degeneration of sexual desire for the spouse and the increase in vicarious fantasy. An example of this is

> the case of a woman of twenty-five who could attain a slight orgasm with her husband if she imagined a powerful older man was taking her by force. Thus the wife imagines that she is being raped, that her husband is not himself but an *other*. The husband enjoys the same dream; in his wife he is possessing the legs of some dancer he has seen on the stage, the bosom of a pin-up girl whose picture he has looked at, a memory, an image. Or he may fancy his wife desired, possessed, violated, which is a way of restoring her lost alterity.[19]

If it were possible to get an open response from married couples of long standing, some vicarious sexual imagery as described above might be more the rule rather than the exception.

One manifestation of vicarious living is a structured over-dependency on our spouse, a need for his or her constant presence and acceptance. This need is often mistaken for love. The intense pleasures produced while being with that one person who is allowed to give such gratifications can be more objectively defined as a dependent attachment rather than a loving commitment. These attachments are possessive and lack the essential characteristics of genuine love—devotion, understanding, and extreme satisfaction in the individuality of the partner.

The effect of all of this is a mechanical, depersonalized interaction between the two people who seem to be controlling and threatening each other, or in the less extreme cases, compromising themselves to maintain the dependency contract. Sexual pleasure and exploration are degraded to a form of "joint masturbation." If they continue to make love to one another, it is in a sense of shame and guilt, for they are aware of their extramarital desires. For this reason the frequency of lovemaking may decrease over the duration of the marriage. For sexual release, each member of the couple may resort to increased independent masturbation in secret. A friend of mine, for example, told me that he masturbated more when he was married than at other times. During his marriage he hesitated to inform his wife of his self-gratification for fear of reprisal. Because of the mechanistic, routine and somewhat frustrating manner in which he related sexually to his wife, he preferred to fantasize, at his convenience and need, that he was having sexual intercourse with his wife's best friend, to whom he was very attracted, and thereby satisfy himself. Many couples, however, cannot admit this kind of repression to themselves, least of all to each other. So they live the vicarious life regarding each other only as a tool for the satisfaction of their needs.

Another problem arises because monogamous norms restrict sexual activity to our spouses. When gratification is not sufficient on the part of one of the couple, frustration results. If this need cannot be satisfied in some manner consistent with the conjugal norms, aggression directed to our mates or to others may develop. Restrictions on sexual expression, far from neutralizing aggression, tend to arouse it, just as the frustration-aggression hypothesis suggests. Sexuality norms function in the monogamous situation when both members are equally demanding of sexual gratification and when monotony and a lack of desire for variety prevail. Not very many couples are able to meet these conditions. Differences in demand for frequency of sexual intercourse and a real desire for a variety of sexual partners (repressed in most couples) places a heavy stress on the monogamous bond.

There is frequent resort to divorce, but within the pretension of monogamy, promiscuous petting outside of marriage, adultery, prostitution, and various other forms of non-monogamous sex relations are quite prevalent. Our monogamy is honored more often in theory than in practice. A. C. Kinsey found that by age 55, for example, one out of two American men engaged in extramarital sex. These figures are conservative because they are so outdated. In a recent study comparing the prevalence of extramarital relations to Kinsey's findings 25 years ago, it was found that young husbands are only a little more likely, but young wives are much more likely, to engage in extramarital sexual activity today. Twenty-four percent of wives and 32 percent of husbands under 25 had done so. Virginia Satir elaborates by pointing out that many people engage in either extramarital affairs or some kind of polygamy (mate-swapping or consecutive marriages).[20]

Monogamy is talk for friends and relatives; polygamy is the reality of our guarded behavior and our subjective feelings and desires. In maintaining the monogamy myth, we have perpetuated the sacredness of the marriage institution and have discouraged experimentation with possibly more rewarding family models. In maintaining the monogamy myth, we have also reinforced a norm that has partly led us to become jealous, possessive, guilt-ridden, self-repressive bundles of anxiety, full of fear and frustration. In confining our mates, we have helped destroy ourselves. The norms which govern this kind of activity surely must be ineffective in part, if not in their totality.

SOCIALIZATION

The process of socialization involves teaching children to become effective participating members of society. The patterns of child rearing have changed to some extent as the family has developed from the extended traditional type to a smaller fragmented form. The new patterns have made the child-adult transition more difficult. The gap between child and adult status is accentuated in the nuclear model and generates considerable difficulties for the adolescent. Among the structural properties of the nuclear family that contribute to these problems, Hans Sebald lists:

1. The limited number of potential adult models.
2. Formation of adolescent subcultures outside the family system.
3. Adult responsibilities being largely invisible to youth.

4. Transfer of guidance and authority from the family to impersonal secondary institutions.
5. Limits of the modern family in meeting needs of belonging and security.
6. Status of the young being achieved by the individual in a solitary fashion.
7. Decline of both the "we" feeling among members of the nuclear family and value indoctrination by the family as a unit.[21]

Perhaps the most significant of these is the first point suggesting the limited number of adult models that children have to learn from. The small size of the nuclear family certainly has some effect upon children's personality and skills. Children being reared in the nuclear family quickly develop a high dependency upon their parents in general and their mothers in particular. This overdependent relationship is detrimental to children for a number of reasons.

It first allows for parental biases to be narrowly imposed upon children. Talcott Parsons, a leading sociological theorist, has pointed out that in an achievement-oriented society like the United States, parents tend to foster high-level achievement motivation. This is brought about by the increased leverage that the parents have as a result of the child's extreme dependence upon them. As a result of the conditional love of the parents —conditional upon achievement in school and peer situations—the child develops a strong motivational commitment to achievement.[22]

Thus, parents inject narrow biases upon children attempting to make them in many cases into something which they themselves have failed to realize. In the more extreme cases, parents relate to their own children in a somewhat "vampiresque" way.

They feed on the child's accomplishments, sucking sustenance for their pale lives from vicarious enjoyment of his or her development. In a sense this sucking is appropriate since the parents give so much—lavish so much care, love, thoughtfulness, and self-sacrifice on their blood bank. But this is little comfort for the child, who at some point must rise above his guilt and live his own life—the culture demands it of him, and after all, a vampire is a vampire.[23]

Because of this restricted and exploitive manner by which parents impose motivation upon their children in the narrow confines of the nuclear family setting, it has been suggested that children be left with their parents for infinitely less time than at present. One alternative is for their studies and diversions to be carried on among other children, under the supervision of adults whose bonds would be more impersonal.

Another bias imposed upon children is their limited exposure to adults of different age groups. Parents are usually between 20 and 35 years of age during the child-raising period. When children are in their formative years, they tend to get little exposure to teenaged, middle-aged, and elderly people. Older siblings and grandparents may serve temporarily in this capacity but they are becoming less available with the increased fragmentation and mobility of the modern family.

As the size of the family decreases—a trend I already noted—children are raised in an environment which fails to prepare them for parenthood. Many parents feel that they themselves are not prepared to raise a family, since they grew up in relatively small families and had very little experience caring for younger brothers and sisters. The trend toward smaller families produces inadequate training grounds for effective parenthood.

Another trend relevant to effective child rearing is the steady increase in the percentage of working mothers. In 1940, for example, approximately 4 percent of married women with children of their own at home under the age of six were working; by 1963, this figure had risen to 22.5 percent.[24] With the increase in the percentage of working mothers, children are increasingly being turned over to baby-sitters and day-care facilities. The poor qualifications of most baby-sitters are rather obvious, and although studies have shown that existing child-care centers are adequate as perceived by mothers, the number of centers available is grossly inadequate. In 1958 only 2 percent of the children of working mothers in the United States were getting group care away from home, and 8 percent were getting no care whatsoever but were left to run the streets.[25] What this amounts to is the growing inadequacy of the nuclear family and society to provide healthy supervised socialization for its children.

Now, let's turn to the effects of the socialization process upon the mother. Most mothers still do not work. Motherhood in these cases is an 18-hours-a-day job, unless relieved by baby-sitters or nurseries. The total dependency of infants compels focusing upon their needs without regard to the mother's. The continuous demands of the small child can seem like a prison from which there is no escape but to wait out the years. As the years release the mother from her bondage, they also rob her of her youth. The rising curve of child neglect also may be related to the percentage of increase of early marriages, compounded by the total dependency of the child upon the young mother.

Another question to consider is whether or not mothers are happy with their children. In an extensive study of Detroit parents, it was concluded that more than one out of every ten mothers found the arrival of a new baby more depriving than rewarding. In another pioneer project of marital adjustment, couples with no children or one child rated their marriages significantly happier than couples with two or more children. These findings were confirmed in a later study. In another project, it was reported that the higher the ratio of children per years of marriage, the less satisfactory the marriage experience. Other research has shown that there seems to be increasing marital dissatisfaction as time passes through the child-rearing stages. After the child-rearing period, marital satisfaction increases slightly but never approaches the original level. Research by Gurin, Burr, Pineo, Paris, Luckey, and others as summarized by Mary Hicks and Marilyn Platt revealed a gradual decrease in marital satisfaction over time.[26] Thus, it seems that children fail to bring happiness into the nuclear family. The old myth is not supported by the evidence. Family life instead of providing a favorable setting for parenthood, provides for a gradual decrease in the contentment of parents.

In review, then, socialization in the nuclear family is inadequate in that it:

1. Makes the child–adult transition difficult.
2. Limits the number of adult models for children to follow.
3. Produces an overdependency of children on their parents.
4. Provides for the teaching of bias of parental values.
5. Allows for an exploitive and vicarious imposition of motivation of the parents upon their children.
6. Confines the exposure of children to people of narrow age ranges.
7. Fails to adequately prepare children for parenthood.
8. Fails to provide adequate parent substitutes when parents are not available.
9. Produces marital dissatisfaction especially in larger families.

3 DISSOLUTION AND FUTILE RESOLUTION

"Don't do anything you may regret" is one of the stupidest pieces of advice ever given. If one took it, one would never do anything at all; to learn something, you have to start by making mistakes and doing it badly—and of course you will regret this later. But this is how one learns.

—John Wilson, *Logic and Sexual Morality*

When our family fails to satisfy our needs, we see stress and tension as the first signs of disorganization. The inherent structure of the nuclear family is most conducive to such tensions. Because this kind of family is propagated along kinship lines, membership is determined by blood or marriage. Our relatives may or may not have common interests and values. When they do not, our family ties hold us together and require our continued interaction. Since our families are not defined along value and interest paths, internal conflict is more likely to result. The exceptions to this, of course, are either when the socialization process is effective in conditioning children to become carbon copies of their parents or when a strong authoritarian parent coerces other members of the family to conform to his or her dictates. In most cases, however, our family members are bound to us in spite of our differences. Our children have no choice as to whom they would like to have as parents and parents are stuck with their offspring who reflect their biology but not necessarily their orientations. What this amounts to is that in a family based upon kinship ties, we can choose our friends but not our relatives. Perhaps being able to choose our relatives as well would be more desirable.

Decision making in the nuclear family is typically limited to the two parents. When only two people participate, democracy is bypassed in favor of an authoritarian partner or a contract based upon compromise.

> A group of two is characterized by high tension and emotion, a high tendency to avoid disagreement, a high potential of dead-lock, a tendency for one to be the active initiator and the other the passive controller with veto—all because of the delicate balance involved in a situation where there is no other support within the group for either participant in the case of disagreement and where getting along is necessary for survival. The prime example, of course, is the husband and wife.[1]

When a couple disagree, there is no majority rule. To allow our children to become involved in making decisions for the family would mean turning the control over to them whenever the parents were in opposition. This seems to be clearly outside of the values of most nuclear families. Parents tend to hold tight to the reins of the family. They choose to retain the right to control their children and to settle questions of discipline between themselves. Opposition between parents in these cases, however, is not uncommon.

Another source of strain in the family is prolonged illness. Sick people are usually best handled in a professional setting, but with removal from the family they are not able to get the attention and support they may want or need from loved ones. The small nuclear family becomes severely strained by the sacrifices necessary to give enough attention to the sick person. When the father is ill for a long period of time, the family's economic security is threatened and the additional attention he requires from his wife is subtracted from the children. When the children are ill, the mother's attention to her husband is reduced. This is equally the case with the newborn infant because of the almost total demand upon the mother's time. The illness of the mother, on the other hand, requires overtime on the part of her husband, unless other relatives are available.

An additional source of strain in our family is its high degree of geographic mobility. This trend has been held responsible for our children's lack of stability and identity formation. This mobility limits the degree of security and companionship that can be given to our young. The youngster, faced with this dilemma, oscillates between two equally frustrating situations, the ineffective family and the confusing outside world, and fails to derive security from either. This mobility also results in an increase in the number and kinds of family adjustments and crises, and the loss of support by friends and relatives at critical times of stress. Opposition to the traditionally disapproved method of solving problems (divorce) is weakened.

For these and other kinds of stress to be relieved, the family system must be altered. Without modifications, the family is likely to become even less effective. Refusing to acknowledge these ineffective structures and processes can, and actually does, lead to increased dissatisfaction and disorganization in perhaps our most crucial institution.

Reason for divorce

DIVORCE

Perhaps the strongest evidence supporting the failure of any social grouping is its rate of dissolution. When institutions are not performing the functions they were designed for, nor satisfying the needs of the membership, severe strains and disorganization would increase. This is obviously occurring in the nuclear family.

Since 1870, the rate of increase in divorce has been consistent in the United States. The number of marriages ending in divorce increased from one in 33 in 1870 to one in four in 1960 and about four in ten in 1970. The latest government figures show a divorce rate of over 46 percent for the first half of 1973. It should be over 50 percent in the near future.[2] This trend, however, is not peculiar to the United States. Divorce rates have been rising in all Western countries. Perhaps the most important factor contributing to the higher divorce rates is the lessened disapproval of divorce itself. It is rather obvious that in areas where divorce is easily obtainable, the rates are higher. In California, for example, where "irreconcilable differences" is all that is needed as grounds for divorce, there is already one divorce for every two marriages. A recent survey indicated that in an affluent community like San Mateo, California, seven out of ten marriages fail.[3] If divorce decrees were as easy to obtain as marriage licences, the rates might become astronomical. When we must place restrictions upon divorce, we should wonder about the amount of contentment and satisfaction the institution of marriage really has to offer. The growing ineffectiveness of marriage and the nuclear family is reflected in the increasing proportion of people desiring divorce as grounds become more liberalized.

The increasing divorce rate is also tied to the emancipation and the egalitarian status of women. When women are not solely or mainly dependent upon their husbands for subsistence, divorce is relatively easy and frequent.[4] Welfare aid and the increase in job opportunities for women, along with their social emancipation, have provided them with enough independence both economically and psychologically to function adequately without the presence of a husband and father.

Another type of family disorganization is separation. The population characteristics of the United States revealed that in 1972, 1,119,000 married men and 2,083,000 married women were separated.[5] Desertions, which would further increase the proportion of unstable families, are not recorded anywhere. All in all, the prospects for patching up the nuclear family, even considering "open marriage," seem rather dismal.

Although more and more couples are turning to divorce, many choose to remain married. If the family structure is so ineffective, why do the majority of married people still stick with it? It certainly isn't because they haven't considered divorce. In an interview with hundreds of married pairs, it was learned that approximately 80 percent of the couples had seriously considered divorce at one time or another, and many of them still thought about it frequently. Only children, poverty, religion, or a lack of courage blocks the decision to get divorced.[6]

Let's further examine some of the reasons why couples choose to remain married. First, do couples really stay married because of their children? In the recent past, reports showed that about two-thirds of the couples getting divorced were childless; one-fifth had only one child. It is rather obvious that the longer couples stay married the more likely they are to have children. Many people might not stay married long enough to have many children. A more reasonable explanation of the relatively small number of children having divorced parents might be that strong family norms encourage unhappy couples to stay together for the children's benefit—even if they can't tolerate their mates. The number of people remaining married is due primarily to these pressures channeled through their relatives, friends, and religious affiliations. The trends reducing these pressures, on the other hand, may partially account for the growing rate of divorce.

Perhaps another major reason why people who are dissatisfied with each other do not get divorced is the lack of an attractive alternative to marriage.

The economic factor must also be taken into account. Divorce rates within the lower classes are higher than those in the upper classes. High income husbands are likely to pay more to support their wives after separation, and wives of upper status families would tend to drop in their standards of living after separation, as well as in the status they acquired through their husband's occupation. Thus, it is advantageous in terms of economics and status for both husbands and wives in the upper class to use restraint in getting a divorce.[7] In the lower classes, on the other hand, the added burden of money problems places increased strain on the marriage. Instead of going through the costly process of divorce, the low income husband commonly turns to desertion.

Many marriages which are unsuccessful are never terminated legally. They are counted as successful marriages because they never show up in any other category. These unsatisfactory marriages have been referred to as *holy deadlock* marriages.

> It may be that there are more holy deadlock marriages than there are divorces. We just don't know how many American marriages are of the "shell" or "facade" type.[8]

In a survey of upper-class married couples, for example, two-thirds of the marriages had become *facade* marriages in the middle and later decades of life.[9]

The effect of divorce on the couple is an increase in suffering in many areas. William Goode, a noted family sociologist, indicates some of these hardships:

1. The cessation of sexual satisfaction.
2. The loss of friendship, love, or security.
3. The loss of an adult role model for children to follow.
4. The increase in the domestic workload for the remaining spouse, especially in the handling of children.
5. The increase in economic problems.
6. A redistribution of household tasks and responsibilities.

The higher suicide rates among the recently divorced and widowed might partly be due to these kinds of difficulties and frustrations.[10] The problems seem to stem in part from the lack of any structural arrangement for postdivorce adjustment. The divorced person is neither single nor married, and the former wife's and husband's obligations to each other are not easily determined. Though the father may have legal obligations to his children, he may see them so seldom that he refuses to obey even these commitments.

Thus, due to the inherent problems of marriage and the nuclear family, greater proportions of families are being dissolved, and the victims are left hanging with no structural support to help them through their difficult period of adjustment. In addition, the individual is still being blamed for marriage failure. William Lederer and Donald Jackson, leading authorities on marriage, state that one of the most apparent causes of divorce is the failure to pick a suitable mate.[11] How ineffective will these institutions become before we stop using the individual as a scapegoat and start looking at the social causes of family disorganization?

If, on the other hand, these institutions are in fact inadequate, then maybe the increasing divorce rates should be looked upon as being a favorable trend. There is little reason to believe that a highly tolerant attitude toward divorce will mean the decline of our civilization. The only necessity is that some sort of social machinery be devised for rearing our children properly. Our options seem to be either to shift the function of socializing children to professional groups and organizations or to seriously consider the creation of new family forms which will meet the needs of people and perform their delegated functions more effectively. Some of these new family forms will be reviewed in the next chapter, and the structural characteristics of my view of the family of the future will be elaborated in Chapter 7.

THE ONE-PARENT FAMILY

Divorce generally leaves children with only one parent. As of 1960, about one household out of ten in the United States was headed by a woman; in 1971, it was less than one out of nine. Six million children are growing up in fatherless homes. In 1966,

Benjamin Schlesinger published an annotated bibliography of 43 books, articles, and research, most of which dealt with problems arising in no-father families. One writer conservatively estimated that 25 to 35 percent of all American parents perform child-rearing roles alone at one time or another under abnormal circumstances.[12]

A surprising fact related to this is that the number of people living alone is increasing much more rapidly than the sum population of the United States. Since 1960, approximately one-third of all new households contain but one person. A reasonable hypothesis suggests that the primary reason for this increase is the persistence of the small nuclear family form.[13] We have no viable alternative family institutions to choose from. We have no other choice but to live alone—except in sin, of course!

Problems which arise in the one-parent families are numerous. For the mother, a dependency on public funds may produce economic burdens and leave her with a sense of inadequacy. Finding competent baby-sitters during working hours or during evenings out can be extremely difficult. Being the head of a household is a demanding, 18-hours-a-day, seven-days-a-week, 365-days-a-year job. During illness the child-rearing problems become intensified when no father is available.

> It is true that the termination of the marriage has reduced or eliminated the mother's role as wife, but she is still a woman in the early decades of life and men will be in the picture sooner or later. Thus she may not be a wife at the moment but she will soon be a girl friend, and the courtship role may be even more demanding than that of wife.[14]

The father has problems too. He has the desire to leave his wife, but he wants the attachment to his children. This dilemma can cause many problems between him and his ex-wife as to the desired manner in which the children should be treated.

Whereas the mother still has the companionship of the children, the father is left alone to start a new life. The period of adjustment immediately following separation can be quite frustrating as well as isolating. Although he doesn't have child-rearing responsibilities, the needs of warmth, esteem, and identification that were satisfied by his children are now neglected. Alcoholism and loneliness commonly result. Thus, neither of the divorced parents gains; both remain frustrated until new relationships develop and then perhaps the cycle begins again.

One of the most documented effects of broken homes is child delinquency. For example, relatively more criminals and delinquents come from broken homes, from broken marriages, and from families that have moved around, than from unified, socially integrated, stable families.

> . . . children from widowed or widowered homes are almost 50 percent more likely to be delinquent than those from intact homes. But children from "separated" homes are over-represented *still more:* The chance that such homes will produce a juvenile delinquent (holding class constant) is almost twice as high as the likelihood that an intact home will produce a juvenile delinquent.[15]

One piece of research suggests a tie between the intense behavior connected with delinquency and the environment of the one-parent home. It was found that in homes with only one parent, children held more intense opinions and were more likely to act upon them.[16] This is further support for questioning the value of an increasingly smaller nuclear family, particularly the one-parent family, in which problems are intensified. The trend is toward an ever smaller number of parent figures with which children can identify. A reversal of this trend, toward multiple parentage, might better satisfy children's needs. We are again invited to reconsider an extended structure—but not necessarily one incorporating kinship and marital ties. The communal family, based instead on friendship ties, will be explored in the last few chapters.

REMARRIAGE

If the nuclear family is as ineffective as suggested, the one-parent family is even more so. But what are the alternatives? Society leaves little room for the nonmarried. Divorced mothers especially have many difficulties living alone. There are, therefore, many pressures on the divorcee to remarry. Among these are greater social approval, a new father for the children, economic security, pressures from relatives and children, and the taboo against sexual pleasure outside of marriage. Most formerly married people have seen remarriage as the only possible solution. The proportion of families resulting from second, third, fourth, and subsequent marriages is on the increase. The figures available indicate the chances to remarry have increased markedly, particularly for young women. Ninety-nine out of 100 women who are divorced by 25 will eventually remarry. Two generations ago only one out of every three divorced people remarried; today four out of five do so. At every age level they are more likely to marry than people who have never married at all, and this difference becomes greater as age increases.[17]

The increasing remarriage rate may be explained by the notion of individual blame for marital failure. Here, when malfunctioning occurs, we are seen as causing it. When our marriage breaks up, it is either our fault or our spouse's. We say that the institutions of marriage and the nuclear family are all right; it was something that we did which led to the divorce or separation. Marital problems are rarely attributed to the inadequate institutional structure. For example, in a recent survey nearly all formerly married subjects believe they know themselves better after a divorce and have a clearer notion of what sort of person they need; virtually all plan to avoid the sort of person they chose before.[18] Our answer seems to be to find another person. It rarely occurs to us to find another institution—or at least make some modifications in the old one.

But does remarriage, as a result of these notions of finding the *right* spouse, actually work? Is our answer really in the proper selection of a new mate? If it is so, then there would be a lower divorce rate for those who have tried marriage a second time. This is not born out: this divorce rate is higher than that for first marriages.

The effect of remarriage on children is not good either. One study revealed children whose mothers remarried appeared to be more emotionally disturbed than those whose mothers did not remarry.[19] Remarriage does not seem to be the answer. It is a prolongation of an outdated institution, an illness of which we have only managed to treat the symptoms.

But life goes on. We continue to marry, get divorced, blame ourselves or our mates and then turn around and get married again. The cycle continues at an ever-increasing rate and we continue to mistake the symptoms for the disease. We search for the sickness in ourselves and our spouses, never stopping to consider the possibility that our "sacred" institution is at the core of the problem.

AWAY FROM FAMILY CONTINUITY

Increased industrialization, communication, and mobility have taken people away from their families and traditional ways of life and have put them in touch with new ways. A more transient society is becoming a reality. Industrialization seems to be associated with a growing disinterest in marriage as a life style, especially by women. The proportion of women who never marry is much greater in modern industrial societies than in primitive or developing ones. As women become more emancipated, a trend which will probably continue, they tend to become more interested in occupations other than motherhood and feel less pressured into marriage and family relationships. Where women have more nearly achieved equal status with men through social, political, and educational freedom, fewer of them end up married.

Increased mobility, transportation, and communication also allow people to come in contact with a greater number and variety of potential mates. In his description of the *permanent-availability* model, family theorist Bernard Farber suggests that each individual, regardless of marital status, is available as a potential mate to any other individual at any time.[20] He presents statistical data and concludes that the evidence supports the application of his model to American society. Thus, with increased mobility and the greater availability of potential mates, an increase in our rate of mate turnover is expected. Our growing divorce and remarriage rates suggest that this is in fact happening. The norm is shifting from monogamy to serial monogamy, and this, in turn, is contributing significantly to family discontinuity and instability.

Our family lacks continuity in other ways. The life of our nuclear family is limited to about 25 years of child rearing and 25 thereafter as the children leave home and begin a new unit. The duration or cycle of our family lasts from 20 to 60 years; then as the parents die, our family dies. Family life today does not always include children, teenagers, parents, and grandparents interacting in a totality. It is, at any given time, just one stage in a cycle of progressive stages. With the continued fragmentation of the nuclear form, these different stages of our family cycle are rarely seen at one time in any one family. Our family as it exists is but a part of the complete family picture. This lack of continuity and wholeness forces parents to anticipate their eventual loss of function. They can expect, as the cycle ends and with the children reared, to be "put out to pasture" to find ways to occupy their "long empty days ahead."

Retirement for the elderly increases feelings of social isolation and loss of function. This problem is becoming more severe in that the percentage of population over 65 years of age increased from 4 percent in 1900 to about 10 percent in 1970.[21] The rather abrupt loss of child-rearing functions on the part of the aged is but another example of how the nuclear structure inherently results in discontent and discontinuity.

The evidence presented above supporting the ineffectiveness of monogamous marriage and the nuclear family is inconclusive, one-sided, open to other interpretations, and incomplete. There are arguments and research findings that could be used to build a case for the effectiveness of these institutions. A critique of this critique is, therefore, inevitable and necessary. But I think that a systematic review of the functioning and structure of marriage and the family, however inadequate and one-sided, is badly needed. The case for the other side, also inadequate and one-sided, has been presented much more in the literature. Let the reader weigh the evidence; the prosecution rests.

4 INADEQUATE ALTERNATIVES

Pessimists tell us the family is racing toward oblivion—but seldom tell us what will take its place.

In our family forms, as in our economics, science, technology and social relationships, we shall be forced to deal with the new.

—Alvin Toffler, *Future Shock*

I maintained in the first three chapters that interpersonal problems should be seen more as a function of poor institutional structuring than as a function of individual personality. More specifically, my basic argument rests upon the proposition that monogamy and the middle-class nuclear family in America today are not structured in a manner conducive to a healthy and rewarding way of life. The many failures of each of these outmoded institutions were illustrated. The structural characteristics which are most ineffective are summarized below:

1. *The small size of the nuclear family,* limiting security and selection of intimate relationships.
2. *Strong kinship ties,* defining relationship patterns and providing the basis for control and manipulation of the young.

3. *Sex differences in the role structure,* restricting certain duties, activities, and emotions to either males or females.
4. *Monogamous norms,* limiting the development of plural sources of sexual-emotional gratification.
5. *High residential mobility,* causing many strains on the family as it readjusts to new environment.
6. *The dependency of the family on the stability of the marriage,* placing the welfare of the children subordinate to the compatibility of the parents.
7. *The temporary nature of the nuclear structure,* producing a lack of continuity over generations, thus excluding the elderly from family participation.

A variety of effects have evolved as a result of these structural characteristics being institutionalized. I have discussed many of them and provided some evidence for their evolution. I see them as the reflection of poor social structuring in our society which in turn has produced, among other things, insecurity, frustration, hate, jealousy, loneliness, and self-alienation. Below, I attempt to summarize the vast number of effects which the monogamous marriage and nuclear family structures have upon the individual. This list is undoubtedly incomplete and hypothetical in some cases; but it will suffice to make the point.

1. Conventional marriage demands total and permanent involvement between two people.
2. Marriage leads to mutual overdependence and restricted gratification.
3. Marriage implies a more or less monotonous day-to-day living together.
4. Romantic love is not indigenous to everyday marital domesticity.
5. Marriage changes romantic love to dependent, possessive, and jealous love.
6. Unhappiness tends to increase with the length of marriage.

7. Behavior in marriage is based largely upon rights and duties rather than spontaneous urges.

8. The stability of marriage is a function of decreasing attractive alternatives outside of marriage.

9. The stability of marriage is a function of the couple's isolation from competing primary loyalties.

10. Marriage, in isolating the couple from other social contacts, tends to produce loneliness and despair, especially for the middle-aged housewife.

11. Kinship ties allow the elders to control the young, using inheritance and other economic sanctions.

12. Mate selection is restricted by elders to the extent to which kinship ties are tightened.

13. Friends take second place to relatives in the obligation hierarchy.

14. Children from families in which fathers have low or no income are economically discriminated against.

15. The small family leads to parental possessiveness of children and to greater child-parent tensions.

16. Adult role models are commonly limited to only one adult male and one adult female; in many cases, to only the female.

17. The increasing fragmentation of the nuclear form provides the minimum amount of genuine care for children and an increasing amount of superficial and temporary involvement as they are left in the hands of baby-sitters and day-care centers.

18. Sex-role differences alienate half of each person's human potential, block cross-sex empathy, destroy the possibility of intimacy, and detract from satisfying sexual relationships.

19. Individuals supporting conventional sex-role differences tend to be more prejudiced, authoritarian, schizophrenic, and dogmatic and have less self-esteem and self-autonomy.

20. The isolated domestic role of the female leads her to

gratification through fantasy, an overdependence upon her children, and a materialistic outlook.

21. Family continuity is seriously interrupted when the father is called away to fulfill occupational or military obligations.

22. The family fails to provide a strong father-child bond, due to the occupational demands of the father.

23. The stability of the family is contingent upon the sexual compatibility of the parents.

24. Monogamous norms do not allow for alternative sources of sexual-emotional gratification when the primary source is unavailable.

25. Monogamy leads more to a dependent attachment than to a loving commitment.

26. Adult work and responsibility are largely invisible to children.

27. Guidance and authority for children in many cases are transferred to impersonal secondary institutions.

28. The fragmented family leaves a little sense of "we" feeling and an inadequate gratification for belonging needs.

29. Children's overdependency on their mothers allows for a bias inculcation of values and motives.

30. Children are limited in their exposure to adults and children of different age groups.

31. Children in small families are not being prepared for parenthood roles, due to their limited experience in caring for younger brothers and sisters.

32. Larger numbers of children in the nuclear family are associated with unhappy parents.

33. In most cases, child rearing is an 18-hour-a-day job for the mother.

34. The kinship system allows no choice for children to select parents, brothers, sisters, and so on; whom one relates to is a function of biology rather than common interests.

35. The family cannot function as a democracy when only two adults share the power.
36. Illness of one family member places a great deal of strain on the remaining members.
37. The geographic mobility of the family loosens support provided by other primary groups, limiting the members' security and companionship, and requiring them to make a variety of adjustments.
38. The divorce rate is steadily increasing, indicating a general growing dissatisfaction with the marriage institution.
39. Family norms support pressures for couples to stay together when they have children, regardless of how unhappy they are.
40. There are no structural arrangements for postdivorce adjustment.
41. The fragmentation of the nuclear family is producing an increase in the percentage of people living alone.
42. The nuclear form fails to provide an ongoing situation in which there are members of various age groups continuously participating in family activities.
43. The family fails to provide an ongoing stability and security for members over generations.
44. The family fails to provide a major function for parents once the children have grown up and started their own families; older couples are left in isolation without respect, responsibility, and authority.

Not all of these effects occur in all families; most of our families can, however, be characterized by many of them. In many cases couples modify the general structure so as to ease some of the symptoms. Although carefully planned changes can work to make marriage and family life more tolerable, the basic elements persist in the vast majority of our households. Our customs, our values, and even our architecture limit experimentation with new family forms. We have gotten into the habit of trying to adjust to the present structure, and attributing our unhappiness to our inability. So our old family form goes on unchanged and we become entrapped by our "normal" neurosis. We tend to see marriage and the nuclear family as the only means to obtain interpersonal fulfillment. This is not too surprising, once we become aware of the fact that alternative structures do not exist, or at least are not readily available to the average person. We are in a bind.

The result of all of this has *not* been the decline of the nuclear family but rather the proliferation of its fragments. More people are getting married and remarried. Monogamy is only changing to serial monogamy. Parents become step-parents and children are more frequently being shuffled around among baby-sitters, day nurseries, grandparents, and weekend fathers. More and more couples are going to marriage counselors and family therapists to find out what is wrong with themselves. Not really understanding the problem, we typically turn to drugs, or alcohol, or television, or some other form of escape. We seem to turn everywhere except to where the problem really is. We just can't imagine that our institutions are at the root of our troubles. We do not seem to understand that institutional structures are man-made, are imperfect, and can be altered. So, rather than modifying the structures, we patch up each other. The problem is spreading, and we continue to treat the symptoms rather than attempt to find the cure. But what else is there to do?

PERMISSIVE MONOGAMY

Some alternatives to traditional monogamy have been suggested and, in various experimental settings, implemented more or less successfully. Several of these innovations involve no substantial change in the basic structure of monogamy itself. They allow for more flexibility in that some alternative approaches to marriage are actually available, but the attempts to institutionalize more workable structures seem to have little effect. Most of the arguments against monogamy still seem to hold no matter how many ways we can become monogamously married or define our marriage as being *open*.

Many states, for example, have liberalized their divorce laws so as to allow for easier dissolution of unhappy marriages. This seems to have helped raise the divorce rate and also increased the remarriage rate. Monogamy still prevails but instead of the traditional pattern in which each person remains with one spouse for life, we now have a trend toward what is referred to as *progressive, sequential,* or *serial* monogamy in which an individual has only one spouse at a time.[1]

Another proposal for preserving the prevailing marriage and family forms was suggested by popular anthropologist Margaret Mead. She suggested that marriage should occur in two steps, the first stage being *individual marriage,* in which two people are interested in an ethical bond meeting their personal needs and the second stage being *parental marriage,* in which children and economic concerns would be added.[2]

Other proposals portray marriage either as a legal contract, renewable following an agreed duration, or as a nonlegal voluntary association.[3] These innovations are token and do not significantly alter any of the ineffective properties of the nuclear family. They may aid in the prolongation of the present system but prolonging an ineffective system only deters us from making the needed major changes.

An individualistic model for extending the marital bond to include extramarital relationships is proposed by Lonny Myers. She maintains that marriage should allow for personal growth through *compartmentalizing* our life. During one segment of time, each spouse would have the opportunity to do things, sexual or nonsexual, that the other spouse would not know about. Both would act according to their conscience and with no accountability to one another for time or energy. This would allow spouses to accept the possibility of extramarital relationships without having to know the degree of intimacy or involvement. In this model, dating after marriage (with or without sex) would be accepted as a legitimate source of personal fulfillment and growth.[4]

Another indication of a significant modification in the monogamous norm is the practice of *mate-swapping*. Swinging, as it is popularly known, involves the exchange of mates for a few hours for the purpose of sexual variety. Perhaps two million individuals have engaged in mate-swapping.[5] In that this kind of arrangement tends to be superficial and short-lived, it adds little to the general effectiveness of the family. Many of its proponents, however, assert that this kind of practice does make marriage more tolerable and interesting and thus contributes to its stability.

Robert Rimmer, the author of the highly controversial novel, *The Harrad Experiment,* proposes another innovation in the marriage institution. He refers to it as *synergamy.*

> Synergamy would be a formal, committed, church-sanctioned marital relationship which can be embraced not so much as a legal form of marriage but as an emotional commitment, preferably in the form of a church ceremony that would give an ordinary adulterous or marital relationship a status approximately equal to the first marriage commitment. In a perfectly operating synergamous marriage, the spouses would enter into one secondary commitment that would take responsibility for any additional children, and would enlarge, not destroy, the original monogamous marriage. The second spouse would live in the home of the primary spouse a portion of the week—one, two or three days—and accept love and involvement in the primary relationship.[6]

This arrangement is a modification and proposed institutionalization of what has been referred to as an *open-ended marriage.* Others agree that supplementary relationships add to and intensify the central relationship.

Edward Hobbs also proposes a model from a theological perspective that seems to fit into this general category. He argues for a *dialogue-centered marriage* where sexual attraction and promiscuity would not be significant in maintaining the stability of the family.

Sexual relationships would not be limited to the marriage bond in any special way whatever, except of course that pregnancy-control would be utilized at all times outside the marriage, and always within it except when children are planned as a result. The primary kind of attraction between the couple, and the primary basis upon which their relationship would be founded and developed, would be centered upon the matter of *dialogue and openness,* a willingness or even eagerness to share oneself —ultimately to the greatest possible extent—with the other person, to expose oneself and one's needs and concerns, and to accept the other self and its needs and concerns.[7]

Many varieties of modified monogamy are thus possible and are being tested. It seems only a matter of time before some of these alternatives will become acceptable, institutionalized, and legal. Open marriage, child-free monogamy, contractual monogamy, trial marriage, or just living together under some kind of monogamous norms (*pair-bonded*) — all are becoming more viable alternatives as conventional monogamy continues to be scrutinized.

In some of the forms discussed above, the monogamous norms that limit the development of alternative sources of sexual-emotional gratification are abandoned. Although increased permissiveness in these kinds of relationships meets one of the seven criticisms of the family outlined earlier, the remaining six are still unsatisfied. The nuclear family's small size and dependency on marital stability still place the welfare of the children subordinate to the compatibility of the parents. The temporary nature of the family continues the lack of continuity over generations and the exclusion of the elderly from family participation. Kinship ties could still be the basis for control and manipulation of the young and the family's high residential mobility would still cause strains because of adjustments to new environments. Furthermore, these proposed modifications in monogamy suggest no revision in sex-role expectations. Thus, only one criticism of the nuclear family model is met through the institutionalization of permissive monogamy—and then only in some cases.

One other proposed structural revision related to family life should be noted before considering group marriage. Largely the socialists and some feminist groups have been promoting state-sponsored day-care centers for children so that mothers are given more freedom to work and develop their careers. In this manner, sex-role differences can become minimized as women are emancipated from domesticity. The problem, of course, is that as women are freed from household and child-rearing tasks, the nuclear family loses more of the very little structure it currently has. A new kind of rootless individual is produced, since strong family ties are hardly created when children are dropped off at the center in the morning and picked up in the evening by tired parents. The superficial and temporary attachments which the children would have with professional parents don't seem to add much to their security, and children would be spending less time with their own mothers. Furthermore, the adult-child ratio in the day-care center does not seem to be high enough to allow for a close long-term relationship between the child and the professional parent. In addition to this, the high mobility of the family contributes to the temporary nature of the attachment between the professional caretaker and the children. The freedom of the mother from child-rearing duties in these cases may be advantageous to herself and perhaps even to her spouse, but it seems to occur at the expense of their children. What children seem to need is a few attachments to adults (not necessarily only one of each sex) toward whom they feel close enough to depend upon for support on a rather permanent basis. The day-care center, with its low adult-child ratio and professional orientation, does not satisfy this need.

Proposals have also been made for retired persons to become involved in day-care centers. Although this solves, in some way, the two perplexing problems of providing activities for the elderly and adequate supervision of the young, it fragments the nuclear family even more by reducing its child-rearing function. Under this kind of arrangement the elderly would play the parent role to a greater extent. This may lead to some conflict with the parents as to the proper way of bringing up the children.

GROUP MARRIAGE

Group marriage or *multilateral marriage* is a voluntary group of three or more persons, each committed to and maintaining marital relationships with others in the group. This kind of arrangement attracted the attention of a sizeable minority of respondents to a *Psychology Today* poll. Twenty-five percent indicated interest in group marriage. A research project on multilateral relations found that some group marriages remained together more than five years but the median was 19 months.[8]

New proposals for extended family structures incorporating multilateral relationships are starting to become more popular. Robert Rimmer, in his book *Proposition 31*, pictures two couples along with their children sharing household and child-rearing duties. This story is an extension of the "In Six" group marriage proposed in his earlier work. Another form of group marriage is presented by Gerhard Neubeck. *Co-spousing* is described as two polygamous relationships, where each spouse is allowed to marry one person outside of the otherwise nuclear family. Separate residences are maintained for each household, and thus some conflicts are avoided.[9]

Another variation of multilateral marital relationships is called *comarital*. These relationships involve intimacy with individuals other than the spouse in an open and shared manner. The adjunct relationships are perceived to be constructive to the original marriage and to have an important role in the now expanded marriage. Other forms of small-scale marriage or group sex in communal settings have been tested, have been reasonably common throughout history, and do exist in various parts of the United States and the world today.[10]

Albert Ellis, in reviewing the history of group marriage,

indicates a strong pessimism about its future viability in the Western world. Among its shortcomings he includes the difficulty of finding a group of people who can live harmoniously with each other, the sex and love problems which are almost certain to arise, and the relative lack of interest on the part of females compared to males. He does cite certain advantages of a group marriage:

1. Affords a considerable degree of sexual variety.
2. Widens and enhances love relationships.
3. Increases and intensifies family life.
4. Provides economic and social advantages through cooperative efforts.
5. Adds an experiential quality to human existence.
6. Provides a setting for those who are interested in gaining a sense of the brotherhood of man within a fairly large segment of their surrounding population.[11]

Group marriage, from my perspective, has the additional advantages of providing more than one relatively permanent spouse and more than one relatively permanent adult model of each sex for children. By increasing the size of the family, it thus provides increased security and a wider selection of members for intimate relationships. Group marriage also may contribute to the breakdown of kinship ties and the reduction of sex-role differences. These trends would seem to be more a reflection of the particular form of the group marriage, rather than of group marriage itself.

The arguments against group marriage include, as Ellis hints, placing responsibility for the stability of the family and thus the welfare of the children on the sexual compatibility of several possible combinations of mates. If one person develops a rejecting attitude towards a mate, the whole network of mate relationships can become disrupted, straining the cohesiveness of the entire group. A simple symbolic divorce between two people can thus break up the entire family. A second point which must be considered is the effect upon family stability when one person or a couple must move away because of occupational demands. This could result in the regressive breakdown of the family into two or more smaller units. Intimate relationships among adults and children would be all but terminated, especially if some of the members moved a great distance away. The increasing amount of residential mobility therefore poses perhaps the greatest threat to the continued stability of any group marriage.

One last argument for the inadequacy of group marriage is the systematic exclusion of the elderly. Age grouping in most marriage forms, including the nuclear family and most forms of permissive monogamy, seems to be somewhat limited to the age group of the parents and that of the children. The older generation and the infant age group are eliminated. Group marriage fails to correct this problem unless adults of different ages are brought into the marriage in some way. In this case, the old mating with the young may present some problems. Marriage, whether it takes a dyadic or group form, still implies property rights and restrictions in mate relationships. However, in group situations I see the maintenance of such ritualistic and legalistic contracts becoming progressively unimportant and the cohesiveness of the family unit becoming a function of friendship rather than kinship.

COMMUNES AND COMMUNITIES

Experimental communes ranging from two or three unmarried adults raising children to large-scale extended families or "tribes" have become more and more popular throughout the Western world during recent years. In the United States, small drug communes, formulated with no particular structure in mind, throw people together so they can "do their own thing." They are semianarchic in their practices and members aren't supposed to "put their trip on anyone else." Sexual activity is somewhat unregulated and an overt fear of manipulation is rather apparent. The absence of structure, however, is not as obvious as the participants would lead one to believe, since dress, verbal and nonverbal expressions, musical tastes, ritualism, and modes of behavior are held in common by group members.

Religious thinking has been the foundation of most utopian communities during the course of U.S. history. These spiritually oriented communes have shown extreme variations in terms of sexuality norms. They have ranged from the strictly monogamous norms of the puritans to the free love practices of the perfectionist Oneida Community in upstate New York, which lasted for 30 years during the middle of the nineteenth centry. Today, they vary from conventional monogamy among the "Jesus freaks" to the group-sex love relationships in the *Kerista* movement. There thus seems to be some kind of spiritual justification for any number of sexuality norms.

Growing in popularity are the communes based upon Eastern thought and theology. The spiritual base in these communes tends to center around individual awareness through introspection. Members are trained in self-hypnosis, meditation, chanting, posture, breathing, relaxation, as well as other forms of self-discipline. They are taught to separate themselves from their physical bodies and their senses. They accept the existence of some kind of internal or subjective state which has properties or potential properties of immortality, self-determination, and eternal peace and joy. Such communes seem to appeal to individuals who are sympathetic to existential or phenomenalogical psychology in that they both favor the practice of searching inward for knowledge and believe in the power of individuals in controlling their own destiny. Highly alienated people who are searching for their identity or who are looking for real meaning in life may find these kinds of communes most attractive.

Another theme that appears to be rather common in the contemporary commune movement might be referred to as *naturalism*. The "back to the earth" communities stress the importance of maintaining a nutritious diet and consuming "natural foods"—that is, food uncontaminated by chemical processing. Sometimes these communes manifest a great distaste for corporate farming and for technology in general. In order to reach these objectives, some of them have chosen to move into rural areas and raise their own foods. Because of their limited financial base, in many cases they have to resort to, or regress to, a simple hand-tool economy.

Spiritualism of one sort or another, the use of drugs, naturalism, and an existentialistic orientation are used in different combinations to form the basis of many communes. These groups do not usually remain viable for any considerable period of time. Members of disbanded communes who are more dedicated to group living seek or organize new arrangements in new settings.

Because of their rather temporary or newly formed existence, these kinds of communes are difficult to evaluate. The larger size of these groups would seem to allow for a wider selection of intimate relationships and in many cases the monogamous norms have been discarded. Dean and Gerda Koontz, in their account of life in a commune of 16 adults and seven children, speak as a married couple:

> If the average man could learn to accept the fact that he and his wife can quite possibly come to love other people with intensity on a spiritual level, could free himself of the shuck that there is only One Person In The World For Each Of Us, he would come to see that there is beauty in his wife sharing deep and meaningful relationships with other men *they both love and respect*. He is allowing her more joy than she could have with one sex partner, providing her with a blessing. The wife should come to feel the same about her husband. In the end, their own lives are enriched by sexual variety, intimate intellectual variety, and are broadened emotionally.[12]

In their commune, a kind of courting took place, and people didn't sleep with one another according to any particular schedule. In fact, people could, and did, sleep alone. The effect of this kind of arrangement, according to the authors, is healthy for children; they believe that children who were old enough to know that something was going on knew exactly what it was and, therefore, had no abnormal interest in it. The authors argue that children would end up no worse than they would under traditional child-raising methods.[13]

Some people suggest the rather extreme position that making love itself is good, the more often the better. Perhaps the extreme position in sexual liberty is expressed by John Pflaum, a practicing psychotherapist and a research psychologist, in his new book, *Delightism*. He prescribes "orgy therapy" which is a disavowal of every sexual inhibition. Each member of the group must agree to do anything requested by the therapist. Personal responsibility is abandoned when responsibility for performing forbidden and secret acts, considered by some to be immoral, illegal, and disgusting, is given to the therapist. Anything goes as long as it does not cause injury to anyone.

> The male who is not maintaining an erection may be massaged, at the invitation of his partner, by several others at once who each, in turn, take his organ into their mouths . . . . One girl can be supported by several men, stomach down, bent in a V shape, with her behind raised high and vagina exposed. A line of men and women lick her and have oral sex until she has an orgasm.[14]

Sexuality, in its liberalization and variety of expression, is losing its relation to the family. To some extent it is becoming an institution in itself outside of the context of reproduction and child rearing. Although unrestricted lovemaking is found in some of the communal experiments, this is not necessarily the rule. Other communes, as I indicated before, are much more conventional and play down the importance of sexuality.

Along with the liberalization of sexuality norms, many communes de-emphasize the relevance of kinship ties and traditional sex-role differences. Children are seen as children of the whole commune and women are expected to perform the same kind of duties as men. A variation of this exists in the Israeli kibbutzim where sex-role differences are eliminated to some degree and child-rearing duties are shared by the parents in the evening and communal nurseries during the day and night. The kibbutzim seem to retain some of the properties of the nuclear family in that the biological parents tend to have a stronger bond with their children than any other adults in the community. In this way, kinship ties are perpetuated. The stability of the community, however, does not seem to be threatened by a decision on the part of the parents to separate or divorce, in that the children are housed in communal dormitories and continue to function in the same manner. It is thus questionable whether a kibbutz can be considered a family in any sense of the word. It seems more reasonable to describe it as several seminuclear families coming together as a community in order to share economic, educational, and some child-rearing functions. Thus, it does not differ much from a small rural community in the United States, with the exception of economic cooperation, sex-role differences, and the housing of children in a central unit.

The major structural limitations, then, are the perpetuation of kinship ties, the retention of a basically monogamous system, and perhaps the large size of the community as the primary unit of identification rather than the smaller extended family. A community of several hundred can work effectively in terms of economic cooperation but when it comes to emotional and psychological needs, a large community may be too impersonal. If the kibbutzim were each broken down into smaller extended family units, each more or less independently dealing with children's demands the family aspect of the structure might be strengthened. Literature dealing with the kibbutz as a child-rearing system indicates that children reared in the kibbutzim and children reared in nuclear families did not differ markedly in deviant behavior. But no definite evidence exists that would indicate that the kibbutz method of child rearing would function more effectively than the nuclear family in an urban, industrial environment.[15] Other than these reservations, the kibbutz movement seems to be as effective as the other alternative models discussed.

One last consideration is the utopian community proposed by B.F. Skinner in his novel *Walden Two*. He envisioned a community of about 1200 people living cooperatively, somewhat like a kibbutzim. One primary difference was that each member adhered to the central value of using *behavioral engineering* principles as a means of social control. Punishment was all but eliminated and approval ranged from indifference to mild positive rewarding. Technology and efficiency reduced labor to a few hours a day per member and specialists of all kinds smoothly operated the community. Although Skinner was rather revolutionary in his economic, political, and child-rearing practices, his proposal retained monogamy. Couples, however, were offered the choice of sharing a room or living in separate quarters. Most of them eventually saw the advantage of having a private room.[16]

Walden Two offers a resolution to most of the structural criticisms directed at the nuclear family. It, however, like kibbutzim, seems to promote monogamy and large community size, while failing to provide for intimate primary identifications.

Both of these systems by virtue of their complexity, would have to be located in rural areas. They are obviously not designed for a family life-style which can be readily integrated into a growing urban population. With this kind of restriction, any large experimental community must necessarily sacrifice the cultural and technological advantages which urban areas have to offer.

Smaller experiments with middle-class communes and communal families seem to be increasing in the United States. Interest in uniting these now relatively isolated units into larger organizations or communities within the urban and industrial environment is growing. Frederick Stoller suggests a *network of families*. A bimonthly publication, *Communities,* is the effort of

four communal areas in the United States to integrate independent experiments and offer information on the growth of the
communal movement. Frieda Porat in her book, *Changing Your
Life Style*, envisions a new model for living which she refers to as
the *creative community*. This community would foster various
kinds of new urban life styles attractive to single people, couples, and communal families.[17]

NEW DIRECTIONS

None of the family systems outlined above escapes all of the
criticisms that I leveled against monogamy and the nuclear
family structure. Then, is it possible that a system can exist
which is rationally and systematically designed for the purpose
of maximizing human satisfaction and happiness, and minimizing pain, frustration, and all of the negative emotions? Is it
possible that a family can exist somewhere in an extended form
in which kinship ties are discounted, roles do not discriminate
against women or children, and sexuality norms are designed
for a deep and meaningful sharing of mates rather than for the
possessive and jealous exclusion found in monogamous situations? Is it possible for the location of the family to be more
permanent and not subject to dissolution due to interpersonal
conflict, and for the family to be stable to allow for continuity
over generations in which members can be born, actively participate all their lives, and die?

To meet these demands, new family forms will have to be
designed, with a new morality, a new approach to love and sexuality, and a new basis for interpersonal involvement. In the
remainder of the text I will attempt to present a preliminary
theoretical foundation for such a structure and morality. This
new framework needs much refinement and elaboration, as do
most first proposals. I recognize the lack of extensive empirical
support for many of the forthcoming propositions. Research
and experimentation will surely await them and ultimately determine their viability.

5 A NEW THEORETICAL PERSPECTIVE

> Human beings want incompatible things. They want
> to eat their cake and have it too. They want
> excitement and adventure. They also want safety
> and security. These desiderata are difficult to
> combine in one relationship. Without a
> commitment, one has freedom but not security; with
> a commitment, one has security but little freedom.
>
> —Jessie Bernard, *The Future of Marriage*

A new family structure and morality should be oriented to our needs. The primary objective would be to maximize our economic and emotional security. In doing this our concern should be with understanding our own frustrations as well as those of others and then discovering the kinds of social models which allow for the greatest amount of satisfaction for each of us in need areas such as survival, safety, belonging, and self-esteem. In the development of this understanding, many human feelings and motives which reflect traditional and present-day values must be reconsidered. Notions of security, fear, personal dependency and commitment, jealousy, possessiveness, and love must be accounted for and integrated.

My objective will be to systematically interrelate these rather central concerns and to suggest new propositions which arise from them. These propositions hopefully will aid in building new family forms.

SECURITY

Our security is closely tied to our satisfaction. It is more than just having our economic and psychological requirements met. It is possible to have our needs satisfied and still feel and be insecure. Security seems to be a function of not only the extent to which our needs are met at the present but also the extent to which they will probably be met in the future. We may then feel secure in that we believe that our needs will be gratified as they arise.

Whether or not we are secure is not only a function of our feelings. Our security more realistically is a reflection of the social situation in which we find ourselves and the extent to which we can count on our sources or origins of gratification. False security is then feeling secure but not having these real sources available.

Two questions dealing with security must be asked. First, how reliable are the sources of our gratification in any given need area and, second, how many sources of gratification would we require in order to maximize our security?

To answer these questions meaningfully, it is necessary to examine the exchange of human rewards. Let's begin with this general definition. The extent to which we depend upon another for gratification, or commit ourselves to another for their gratification, is the extent to which we are said to be involved. Our involvement can then take two forms: *dependency* (demand for rewards), or the degree to which we can rely upon another for the satisfaction of our needs; and *commitment* (supply of rewards), or the degree to which another can rely upon us as a source of his or her satisfaction. Simply stated, dependency refers to what we expect from others and commitment is what we are willing to give to others.

DISTRIBUTION OF INVOLVEMENT

There are three general ways in which we can distribute our involvement among others. First, we can centralize our dependency and/or our commitment in just one other person (sometimes referred to as *particularization*). Second, we can scatter our dependency and/or our commitment among a wide range of others, suggesting a superficial kind of involvement bordering upon little or no involvement at all. Third, we can become dependent upon and/or committed to a few others — more than one but not so many that our relationships lack any depth.

What is relevant here pertains to what kind of involvement distribution is most effective in contributing to our economic and psychological health and should therefore be used in building a new social structure. To begin with, we must ask the basic question of how many sources of dependency must we have to be most secure?

One extreme view is that only a single source (one other person, or one job, or one group to identify with) is sufficient for maximizing security. This thinking is reflected, for example, in the monogamous nuclear family, in the people who are qualified for only one kind of job, or in the people who have limited their identification and commitment to the members of their immediate family or to some other small ingroup. At the other extreme, we have people who have many superficial sexual-emotional attachments, interests in so many occupational areas that competency is never achieved in any of them, or a weak commitment to many groups, clubs, or organizations.

Overdependency on one source of gratification (centralizing or concentrating dependency) does not seem to provide the most security. In this case, all of our gratification in a certain need area can come from only one particular source. The removal of that source necessarily implies deprivation and frustration, at least until we can develop another source. In the meantime, we may respond with anxiety and defensiveness and, in more severe instances, with aggression or depression.

The people who are rejected by their husband or wife emotionally or sexually and have no one to turn to; the workers who are fired from their jobs when there is no demand for their kind of skill and they have no qualifications in other occupational areas; the children who, because of divorce or a death of one parent, are neglected by the only adult figure available; the elderly couple who live alone and one of them dies—these are examples of how insecurity occurs and can be quite threatening when we rely upon only one source. Minor variations of these occur quite frequently in our everyday life. As long as the one source is available, all seems to be well, but many of us generally overestimate our ability to readily develop new sources.

I have been confronted with the argument that finding new sources for gratification is not very difficult. This may be the case for those of us who happen to possess the attributes which are in great demand in our society. A young attractive woman, for example, might have little trouble finding a source of sexual gratification, someone who is very aggressive and popular might easily develop a new source of affection, a person who has a millionaire father with a lot of "connections" might have no problem finding another job, or those who are talented in many areas may find sources of esteem and admiration almost instantaneously. But how about most of us who are not pretty, not from a wealthy family, not outgoing, not naturally talented, and may not be of the "right" age, sex, or race? What do we do in the meantime? What do we do when our sole source, our security, is lost? This period can be extremely frustrating and depressing. Having no income, no self-esteem, no affection, no sexual or emotional companionship—these are not the kind of situations most of us would like to find ourselves in—not even temporarily! And the less we are in demand the longer we can expect this period to last.

Developing alternative (plural) sources in each need area seems to be a realistic approach to this *interim insecurity* (the period from when we lose our sole source of gratification to the time we develop a new source). If we had two or more available sources of gratification, the interim period would be nonexistent. When deprived by one source, we would simply move to another. The presence of an alternative source generally decreases or eliminates our period of insecurity. The *feeling* that we have another available source similarly decreases our *feeling* of insecurity. Those of us who are fortunate and have many sources of gratification have a higher probability of continuous satisfaction. If one purpose of our family is to provide maximum security for its members, then our values should promote the development of multisource gratification. Each of us would consciously strive not to become too dependent upon any one role, any one skill, any one interest, any one taste, or any one person for any one need.

As a totally decentralized (superficial) person, on the other hand, we are not to be envied. Our relationships are short-lived, our friendships are shallow, our skills are weak, our tastes are indiscriminate. Our gratifications are of the same nature. We can get a little satisfaction from a lot of people and things but if we are really deprived in a certain need area, we have no one person or thing to turn to. Our lack of deeper commitment to potential sources then tends to be repaid with their lack of commitment to us. The primary appeal of superficial relationships is that if we don't get too dependent upon anyone or anything else, we don't have to risk being rejected. We can rationalize that we don't need other people or other things. In spite of our rationalizations and fears, we remain basically deprived and insecure. We lose a closeness to and a concern for others, and possibly ourselves.

When we decide exactly how many sources are most desirable to develop, many factors must be taken into account. Perhaps the most apparent is the extent to which our sources are reliable; that is, the extent to which we can count on them when they are needed. Their reliability on the other hand is a direct function of the extent of their returned commitment. To get commitment from them generally involves at least these two important concerns: the amount of time we spend with them or on them (implying commitment to them), and the number of immediate surplus rewards they have to offer us (availability).

In the case of the first concern, there is a limited amount of time any of us has to invest in developing commitment. The ideal, of course, is for us to spend a considerable amount of time on several sources and thus to establish many reliable sources. Realistically, however, our choice ranges from spending a great deal of time on a few to spending a little time on many, from having a few very reliable sources to having many unreliable sources. This suggests a dilemma in interpersonal involvement, namely, that *the more sources of gratification we have available, the less reliable they tend to become.* This is an example of the principle of diminishing returns. Ideally, then, the greater the number of reliable sources of gratification we have the greater our security. Realistically, having a few rather reliable sources offers more security than having either many unreliable sources or only one extremely reliable source.

It is possible, however, for us to have many reliable sources of gratification, if these sources are willing to commit themselves without getting commitment returned, or without our spending much time with them. This kind of model for interpersonal involvement necessarily implies that some of us will be extended a great deal of security and others will have less than their share. (It must be kept in mind that dependency and commitment, because they refer directly to supply and demand of rewards, are finite. Thus, it is impossible to construct a system in which everyone has *many* extremely reliable sources of gratification.) This model therefore includes:

1. Developing a few rather reliable sources of satisfaction in each need area.
2. Decentralizing dependency and commitment among these few.
3. Avoiding becoming too dependent on or too committed to any one source.
4. Avoiding extreme decentralization of involvement

among many sources producing superficial and relatively unreliable relationships.

These are the theoretical conditions on which a new humanistic system of interpersonal involvement could be formulated.

Before continuing, it would be appropriate to mention a trend in literary and social writings which suggests that it is possible for us under certain conditions, to reach a point of increased psychological independence from our social milieu.[1] This notion is reflected in such terms as *self-autonomy, transcendence, self-containment, free will,* and the like. This kind of independence, if interpreted as withdrawing from social influences and need-gratifying experiences, presumes that we can to some extent satisfy our own wants, determine our own responses at will, and establish security within ourselves. To me, this line of thinking seems quite untenable. We are *interdependent.* The *independent* people are those whose needs are not met, not because they don't need gratification but typically because the social system does not supply it. They in turn rationalize their deprivation and resort to such mechanisms as fantasy in which they imagine their needs for affection, admiration, belonging, or wealth are overly satisfied. This, of course, is an unhealthy escape from reality.

Our concern, therefore, is not whether independence is better than dependence, for dependence, or rather interdependence, is assumed to be much healthier. Our problem is to decide what kinds of interdependent relationships are more gratifying and more security-producing than other kinds. The distribution of our dependencies and the quality of our personal relationships are thus our proper concern.

Each of us varies in terms of our patterns of involvement with others. Some of these patterns seem to provide for greater satisfaction and more security than do others. Three major types of involvement patterns to be discussed, ranging from least to most desirable, include self-involvement, reciprocal-involvement, and love-involvement.

SELF-INVOLVEMENT

Self-involvement can be defined as the extent to which commitment to others is absent or coerced and dependency upon others varies. It is the extent to which we do not voluntarily supply others with gratification but rather rely upon others to provide it for us. The emphasis in this kind of pattern is on taking rather than giving, on demanding rather than supplying, and on self-gratification rather than the satisfaction of others. Dependency is present but commitment is avoided.

When this kind of pattern prevails, some of us are better equipped to do the demanding, to do the taking, and to retain a larger proportion of the rewards. We generally are able to do so because we happen to be endowed with the kinds of attributes which our respective culture values, whether it is intelligence, maleness, youth, physical attractiveness, whiteness, manual dexterity, or birthright. Others who are not so fortunate as to possess these qualities generally end up with greater deprivations and insecurity.

In terms of interpersonal relations, voluntary commitment is not prominent. When we get commitment, it is usually coerced, demanded, and exploited. Women, for example, are owned and used by men for emotional and sexual satisfaction as well as for the performance of domestic tasks. Our sexual relationships range from rape in the most exploitive form to free love, promiscuity, or strictly controlled ownership of mates as in institutionalized varieties of polyandry and polygyny (harems).

In summary, those of us in a *self-involved* kind of system are not interested in voluntarily committing ourselves to others but are rather preoccupied with forcing total commitment from others through coercion or legal mandates. Self-involvement provides for the overgratification of the few and the undergratification of the many. It is involvement based upon greed rather than need, and it produces the least amount of general economic and psychological security for all of us.

RECIPROCAL-INVOLVEMENT

Reciprocal-involvement can be defined as the extent to which commitment is contigent upon dependency, that is, the amount of gratification which we supply to another is determined solely by the extent to which we can rely upon the other person for gratification. It is a system of investment in which we give in order to get and when we get, we are expected to give as much in return. The emphasis here is on exchange, on balance, and on mutual gratification. It is a system in which each of us has rights and duties, and in which there is competition to get the most for what we have to give. In it, some of us again receive more than others, because we have the resources which enable us to use the rules of the system to our advantage.

In economic terms, it takes the form of the market in which goods, land, labor, and capital are the major commodities for exchange. Buying and consuming are economic consequences of demand and dependency, as producing and selling are functions of supply and commitment. Phrases such as "a day's work for a day's pay" are examples of thought reflecting the norm of reciprocity. Because this system, as compared with self-involvement, is based upon giving as well as taking, material deprivation is less common and general economic security is increased.

In the political structure, justice is commonly based upon the principle of "an eye for an eye and a tooth for a tooth." It might be noted that *lex talionis,* or "balancing the scales" still prevails as the model for dealing with deviance. The amount of punishment people receive is thus directly proportionate to the severity of their offense against society. This kind of model also dominates many religious institutions. Retribution for sins against God is hellfire and damnation, and the amount of penance generally equals the amount of sinning.

In terms of interpersonal relations, reciprocal-involvement implies that such rewards as affection, esteem, help, and encouragement should be given to others only with the expectation of getting some kind of return. The fear of not receiving as much psychological support as we have invested tends to produce caution, restraint, and suspicion in our social relationships. Our failure to maintain ego-balance (getting as much as we give) on the other hand, results in defensiveness, anxiety, aggressiveness, or depression. Responses which follow this kind of deprivation may include belittling, projection, attention getting, withdrawal, rationalizing, fantasizing, and suppression.

Our suffering egos thus drain others of psychological rewards, for we have much to demand and little to supply. We are extremely dependent and cannot carry out our commitments. Since exploitation and force are unacceptable in a system based upon reciprocity, we use persuasion and promise of commitment to get what we need. We manipulate people to our advantage and only return rewards when we are fearful of losing what we have already profited.

Our satisfaction is secured only when at least one of our sources is considered reliable. Our preoccupation in reciprocal relationships is directed to that end. We tend to be primarily concerned with totally committing ourselves to one job or to one person, so as to insure the reciprocal commitment. Thus, we *centralize* our involvement so that whomever or whatever we are largely dependent upon or committed to is also largely dependent or committed to us. As a result, our *other* interests and our *other* interpersonal relationships tend to be rather superficial and unreliable.

Probably the best example of this mutual dependency and commitment is found in romantic love. It goes something like this. We meet someone and begin to spend time together. At first, we extend our commitment to each other by providing our partners with various kinds of need-gratifying responses. These responses soon become so rewarding that they produce a state of mutual psychological euphoria. This process of building reciprocal admiration is commonly referred to as falling in love.

As we continue to spend more time with each other, we begin to spend less time with others. This weakens each of our possible alternative sources of gratification. In ending our dependency on others, we tend to focus or centralize our dependencies on our partner. Since we now have only one reliable source of gratification, we guard it carefully. We become each other's possession, each other's property. As our dependency increases, we also become more aware of the deprivation and frustration which we would experience if we were to lose our "loved one." We are threatened when our partner shows any interest in developing a relationship with anyone else. This insecurity is typically manifested in our extreme jealousy, cloaked with anxiety, and in our threat to withdraw our commitment for fear of rejection. The fear of rejection can be partly attributed to the romantic myth suggesting that it is possible to love only one person. The ultimatum that "either you become totally committed to me or our relationship is over" typically follows—"it's all or nothing at all."

We assume that the extension of commitment to someone else means the withdrawal of our vows. To guard against this danger, we continuously reaffirm our mutual obligation with such utterances as "I love you" and "I need you." This can be interpreted as "I am committed to you" and "I am dependent upon you." More realistically, however, we might say to each other, "I will continue my *commitment* only as long as I can *depend* upon you," or in more romantic terms, "I will love you as long as you love me."

In most cases, verbal commitment is not sufficient in reducing anxiety; therefore we seek legal commitment. We decide to get married. The contract is granted in public ceremony and in effect declares that we are from that time on totally obligated to one another. Neither of us is to develop other sources of this kind of gratification.

When spouses elect to positively reward each other, this behavior can be understood to represent the best means available to each of maximizing individual rewards while maintaining minimal costs. When spouses elect to reduce the rate of positive reinforcement, this too can be understood in terms of the reward-cost balance. In such situations, each spouse has learned from past experience that his rewards dispensed to the other will not be reciprocated and each seeks to conserve his resources. Thus, whether or not one partner positively reinforces the other will be a function of his past experience with the other, while the presence of the reciprocal interaction suggests that: "Each individual has something to offer by way of reinforcing the other, and once established, the interaction sustains itself." [In normal marriage,] each partner has learned that if he positively reinforces the other, he will be compensated in the same magnitude. In effect, each partner seeks to raise the rate at which he reinforces the other with the assurance that the rate at which he is reinforced will rise a like amount.[2]

Well, this works fine as long as each of us provides satisfaction in all of our spouse's need areas. However, if one of us fails to gratify our mate, the whole relationship can become threatening. Because of our total dependency, we, the deprived party, become defensive and retaliate or seek to develop gratification sources outside of the marriage relationship. Since developing an alternative source is not permitted in the contract, when we become involved outside of the marriage we must be deceitful or face the possibility of conflict and divorce. This may result in the loss of our partner, our original source of gratification. Being aware of this possibility, we tend to emphasize and ritualize the importance of honesty in building and securing our relationship.

It is ironic that honesty exists in an atmosphere of rather complete acceptance; that is, we will probably be honest with another to the degree to which we believe that the other person will not withdraw a commitment or will not respond in a punishing manner. Since honesty in this case of extramarital involvement would result in a loss of commitment and in certain sanctions, it would not likely be forthcoming. It seems more reasonable to hypothesize that the more threatening and insecure our relationship is, the more we emphasize and demand honesty, and the more we emphasize and demand honesty, the less honesty will prevail. Our overt declarations of honesty are but facades for our deceit.

Recently an acquaintance informed me how much she "trusted" her spouse. When I asked her what she meant by the word, she thought seriously for a moment and then responded with, "Trust is when two people never catch each other lying." Trusting in this sense seems to involve the ability to cover up real feelings and acts of unfaithfulness. Perhaps when two people feel the need to reaffirm their mutual "trust" continuously, they in fact are only repressing their real feelings and/or behaviors. When they say "I trust you" to their mate, they may be saying to themselves, "I hope I can trust you to remain faithful to me, but I don't trust myself to do the same."

We as "adjusted" couples then continue our lives under the pretense of honesty—"I'll pretend to trust you if you pretend to trust me." This gives our family and friends the false impression that we are genuinely happy and that each of us completely satisfies the other's every need. Can you imagine the number of extramarital fantasies we have and repress for fear of disapproval and rejection on the part of our mates? If, on the other hand, we get caught in a lie or we confess our outside involvement, our relationship becomes tenuous, for very few of us can live in a monogamous situation knowing that our mates are thinking about or having extramarital relationships.

Another variation of reciprocal-involvement which is commonly agreed upon in marriage has to do with the exchange of economic rewards for social and psychological commitment. Generally, when we get married, the man is expected to provide the woman with food, clothing, and shelter. In return, she is expected to render domestic services, including housekeeping and sexual-emotional gratification. In this sense, then, marriage is institutionalized prostitution, at least to the extent to which the wife demands economic payment for sexual services. One of the primary reasons that women get married is for economic security, and one of the primary reasons that men get married is for guaranteed sexual satisfaction.

It is noticeable that sexual partners outside of marriage are more difficult for men to obtain than women, and economic security outside of marriage is more difficult for women to obtain than men. As women become more liberated, both in sexual and economic areas, motivation for marriage would seem to become less distinguishable along sex lines.

Other examples of reciprocal-involvement could be elaborated. A common occurrence is when we invite our neighbors over for dinner and expect to get a return meal before we extend a second invitation. Another case is when the person who buys a round of drinks expects the other members of the party to pick up the tab for the following rounds. Many of us come to a compromise based upon the principle of "we'll do what you want to do, if we can then do what I want to," or "if you buy what you want, I get to buy what I want." In another case, we as parents frequently tell our children that they must complete their chores if they expect to get their allowances.

In these and many more instances, we extend gratification conditionally, based upon the "I'll scratch your back, if you scratch mine" or "you're OK, *if* I'm OK" principle. This is the kind of involvement which dominates most modern societies and sets the rules for give and take. If you don't believe it, try returning a compliment with an insult and count the number of additional compliments you receive. Our egos seem to be in such a delicate balance that we cannot afford to give up much psychological gratification without responding defensively.

In review then, when we are members of a system founded upon reciprocal-involvement, we commit ourselves only when commitment is returned. We give only when we think we can get, and we take with the anticipation of something being demanded in return. To the extent to which discrimination exists in the system, those of us who have favorable attributes tend to get more than we give. As a result, the remaining members of the system suffer relative economic or psychological deprivation.

LOVE-INVOLVEMENT

Love-involvement can be defined as the extent to which commitment exceeds and is not contingent upon dependency; that is, the extent to which we supply another with more gratification than we rely upon the other person to supply us, and we do it expecting nothing in return from that person at that time. It is a system in which the emphasis is on giving rather than taking, on supplying rather than demanding, and on the satisfaction of others rather than of ourselves.

When this kind of pattern prevails, we become highly oriented to the needs of others and are willing to give to them primarily because they are needy. And because we are willing to give without expecting or demanding a return, the gratification of everyone is maximized. It is a process of the economically and psychologically rich giving to the poor so that social as well as psychological class structures are destroyed. Each person is seen as a worthy human being, deserving of sufficient gratification.

In terms of interpersonal relations, love-involvement is an identification with the human race and a sharing of strong commitment among those with whom one is involved. It is not restricted by sex, age, physical appearances, blood lines, or other biologically determined properties. It is meaningfully relating to others without the feeling of being their property or their possession, and without becoming too dependent. It is the breakdown of contractual relationships. It is a modified polygamy (based upon commitment and empathy) rather than polyandry, polygyny, monogamy, or promiscuous superficial free love.

The conditions necessary for increasing love-involvement according to this definition are threefold: our dependency must be minimized, our commitment must be increased, and our commitment contingent upon dependency must be decreased.

Let's also review how some of the involvement patterns already discussed fail to produce love. In Figure 5-1, I attempt to illustrate, using a series of curves, the process of developing an involvement with another when we are *self-oriented*. As we spend a greater amount of time with another, we become increasingly dependent. Seeking only dependency, our commit-

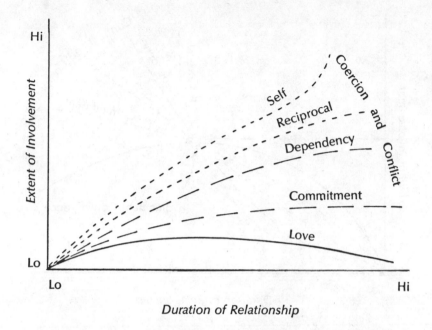

FIGURE 5-1 Self-Involvement in Developing Dyadic Relationships

ment curve is lowered. In failing to extend commitment to others, they in turn tend to be less willing to reciprocate. Getting very little from others, we have little if any to give. We need whatever we have and our dependency curve struggles to maintain even a modest level. The relationships which we do establish are thus exploitive and coercive. Our superficiality in relating to others and our lack of concern for their needs result in the absence of any significant feeling of love for them. Our self becomes primary, our love for others diminishes, and our involvement curves in general assume a rather low trajectory.

In Figure 5-2, I attempt to illustrate the development of an involvement with another when we are *reciprocally-oriented*. Unlike the self-involvement model, we at least begin with the

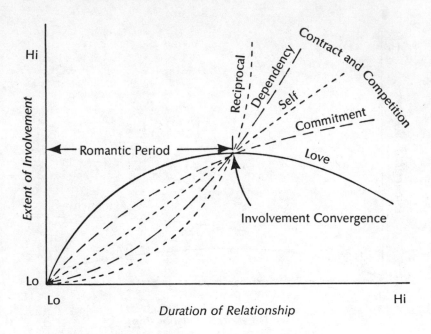

FIGURE 5-2 Reciprocal-Involvement in Developing Dyadic Relationships

notion of giving and receiving rewards unselfishly. During this preliminary romantic period, we extend our commitment to others somewhat beyond their dependency (our reward output exceeds our reward input). At this stage, our love for the other person climbs and surpasses our *self* and *reciprocal* orientation. As we cut off our involvement with others to concentrate on our partner, we centralize our dependencies and gradually lose our alternative sources of gratification. When we become highly dependent upon the one person, our modest unselfish commitment and love evolve into a reciprocally dominated mode. Our commitment continues to rise but now it begins to become conditional; that is, we have overinvested ourselves (our costs) and we begin to take our returns (our gains) for granted and anticipate even greater rewards (profits).[3] When our anticipated returns are not fully realized, we become increasingly threatened due to our overextension of commitment and our lack of alternative sources of gratification. Our self-involvement curve continues to increase and our dependency curve turns sharply upward. Because of this threatening state our commitment and love curves begin to relax and level off. We become cautious in our giving and fearful of not getting back as much as we have invested. Our ever-increasing dependency on the other person places us in a vulnerable position, and we can no longer give without some guarantee that our giving will be reciprocated. At this point, our commitment and dependency curves converge.

The point of *involvement convergence* has significant implications in our relationship. It marks the end of love and the beginning of an exchange involvement. In most relationships, this point is extremely difficult to detect or measure but it does exist. It is witnessed in every case where a relationship begins with romanticism and strong commitment and ends in overdependency, contract, and self-concern. Again, the common example is when we fall in love at first but spend our postnuptial days bickering and bargaining for our respective self-interests. (It should be noted, of course, that a relationship can originate at this point of involvement convergence, omitting the romantic period. Such a relationship is based from the beginning upon a contractual model and is found quite commonly in situations characterized more by economic exchange.)

Following the point of involvement convergence, a period of becoming aware of the rules of exchange occurs (sometimes referred to as romantic disillusionment). This period continues until the contracted rules of our relationship become accepted, well established, and practiced by both parties. It is generally characterized by our heightened anxiety. What threatens us and makes us hypersensitive is the fear that the other person may seek an involvement with a third party. Assuming, of course, that there is rather complete commitment and dependency between us, when we suspect the other person of shifting commitment, we typically respond with increased defensiveness. Our ego is set off balance, and we become intolerant of the slightest criticism in general and any negative feedback from our partner in particular. A perception of shifting commitment, along with any form of rejection from our partner, can produce an extremely volatile situation. Under these conditions, our security is at stake, since our sole source of gratification is seen to be weakening. Since we have no viable alternative, we become more self-oriented and respond in one or more of the following manners to protect our investment.

1. If no alternative sources of gratification are immediately accessible we may respond *aggressively*. We strike out at our partner with verbal or physical attacks. Our rationalization for our behavior is usually founded upon the reasoning that our partner has violated the rules of the contract in some way and is deserving of the assault. Retaliation from the other person can lead to a chronic exchange of degrading responses, or, in the extreme case, to termination of the relationship. If the relationship persists, the negative exchange pattern characterized by belittling, projection, and quarreling becomes a form of institutionalized masochism and we adjust to it as a way of life. The possibility of establishing mutual love fades, and we continue the vicious competition to maintain our own ego-balance. We become "intimate enemies."

2. A second response, when no alternatives are available, is to *compromise*. We introduce refinement of the contract. The new rules center around mutual agreement not to provide further responses to one another which could be interpreted as threatening. What this amounts to is a reaffirmation of our total commitment. Reciprocity is preserved and our ego-balance is maintained. We have adjusted to one another and our commitment and dependency curves run more or less parallel. Commitment, however, never exceeds our dependency. For this reason, we cannot in fact love one another. We may, in lieu of love, expect a periodic "I love you," as well as the giving of gifts

on certain occasions. This behavior is supposed to impress our friends and acquaintances of our mutual concern. We thereby fool others and sometimes even ourselves into believing that our relationship is somewhat ideal. This impression can continue for many years, as long as we follow the established norms of reciprocity which allow us to function without the threat of losing the other. Our love and romanticism of the earlier stages end up in disillusionment and as our relationship continues, we settle down to the realities of an exchange existence.

Writers have elaborated on the self-destructive urges of people caught up in this kind of situation. Denis de Rougement, for example, describes unhappy mutual love in the following manner:

> They love one another, but each loves the other from the standpoint of self and not from the other's standpoint. Their unhappiness thus originates in a false reciprocity which disguises a twin narcissism. So much is this so that at times there pierces through their excessive passion a kind of hatred of the beloved . . . . The essential unhappiness of this love is that what they desire they have not yet had—this is death—and that what they had is now being lost—the enjoyment of life. And yet, far from this loss being felt as privation, the couple imagine that they are now more fully alive than ever and are more than ever living dangerously and magnificently. The approach of death acts as a goad to sensuality. In the full sense of the verb, it aggravates desire. Sometimes even, it aggravates desire to the point of turning this into a wish to kill either the beloved or oneself, or to flounder in a twin downrush.[4]

3. The third response, when no immediate alternative is accessible, is for us to psychologically or physically *withdraw* from the other person (disinvolvement). This response usually occurs when, as the threatened person, we find aggressive tactics unsatisfactory. When overt attempts to regain our ego-balance have failed, our only remaining course is to turn inward into our subjective existence. We isolate ourselves behind barriers which insulate us from further negative input. We suppress

or repress any threats. Our protective layer allows us to create an internalized social system. In this fantasy world, we imagine ourselves to be in a position in which others accept us, admire us, or are in some way sympathetic to our needs.

A friend of mine informed me that when she had been a young girl, she had created an imaginary family. Her family had consisted of her mother, father, and 14 siblings of all ages who liked her very much. Her fantasy family had lasted at least ten years, and its ongoing activities were reactivated daily or weekly, depending upon her time and need. She could name each brother and sister, and describe their physical features and personality characteristics. She had cut out pictures of people from magazines who resembled them but at one point decided to destroy these tangible symbols of her imaginary world for fear that her real parents would discover them. Her escape into herself and her inner family was obviously more rewarding at times than the activities going on around her, for she could control her imaginary family to satisfy her felt needs —something that she couldn't do with her real family.

This kind of escape into ourselves is commonly manifested by depression, despair, and a feeling of psychological and social distance from others. In more extreme cases, it is characterized by elaborate illusions, paranoia, and a loss of social participation. An increasing search for identity, drug usage, and the popularity of existential writings are symptomatic of this growing trend which focuses on introspection and self-order. Schizophrenia is the ultimate effect.[5] Combining the *aggressive* and *withdrawal* responses, we have the classic case of the manic-depressive.

4. Other responses to threatening situations arising from the reciprocal model involve our seeking new sources of gratification. These responses are more realistic, in that they directly deal with the underlying problems of need-frustration and insecurity. As the threatened person, we in effect are saying, "If I can't depend upon you, I'll find someone else to satisfy me." Under a contract of total involvement between two people, this

response can be most anxiety producing. Since the developing of alternative sources of satisfaction produced the original threat, this behavior is highly unacceptable. Our new involvements, therefore, because they must be pursued in secret and when the time is available, tend to be superficial. They may provide us with some additional security, but if discovered, may jeopardize the security established in our primary relationship. As I already noted, this kind of situation abounds in suspicion, jealousy, and competition for possession. Our practice of the *double standard* is an appropriate example.

This double standard is commonly manifested when one person is monogamously married or bonded to someone else and the second person is free to pursue a relationship. I have been acquainted with several of these involvements. Those people who are overcommitted to their spouses must cautiously schedule meeting times and places with their lovers so as not to be discovered. The other person must adjust his or her life to meet the needs of the married partner. The free partner's needs are of little concern in this relationship, for the married partner may or may not be available when these needs are most deprived. It tends to be a one-way relationship, in which the married partner practices the double standard. The relationship usually assumes a superficial character with the only real advantage being sexual variety. In many situations the free partner will also take on the role of therapist in that he or she is in the position to discuss the partner's family or marriage problems. This kind of involvement hardly means security for the free partner, for the relationship would probably be ended abruptly if suspicion were aroused or if actual discovery by the spouse occurred. What must be rejected is the tyranny of the double standard when it is imposed upon those who repudiate it for their own lives and see its destructiveness on those who are kept ignorant of other options.[6]

In review, then, it can be seen that neither aggressiveness, nor compromise, nor withdrawal, nor superficiality produce love. Each of these responses, although varying to some degree, still generally follows the reciprocal model. Aggressiveness, because of its destructive and exploitive nature, has the effect of maximizing our dependency and minimizing our commitment. Compromise is also characterized by our dependency exceeding our commitment but perhaps to a lesser degree. Withdrawal comes a little closer to meeting the conditions for love-involvement, in that our dependency is reduced. Our commitment is also reduced, however, and, although the two curves may approximate each other, rarely can we extend our commitment beyond our dependency.

Among the four possible patterns, love is most likely to occur when superficial involvements accompany our primary reciprocal relationship. Our dependency on the primary relationship in this case is reduced, which in turn makes it less threatening. This decreases the distance between our dependency and commitment curves and allows our commitment to become more dominant. The relative increase in our commitment meets a condition for love-involvement, and would therefore promote a greater concern for the needs of the other party. If this is so, the married woman who had a lover or two besides her mate would be able to love her husband more than if she had no other lovers. It is difficult for married couples in a reciprocally oriented society to accept these additional involvements. The myth of "you can only love one person" rather obviously contributes to our overdependency on the one person and curtails our extension of a meaningful involvement to second and third parties.

I might in summary offer this generalization which tends to offend the romantic but expresses the sense of this discussion. *The extent to which we are dependent upon another is the extent to which we tend to be less concerned with their needs and more concerned with ourselves.* Holding our commitment constant, the more we need someone else, the less we can love them. Reciprocal-involvement, because it encourages our overdependency, thus stifles our concern for others. Conventional marriage, as an example of such an involvement, can then be seen as destroying rather than promoting love.

I have argued that reciprocal-involvement fails to produce love. The following propositions are offered as support for this position.

1. Reciprocal-involvement produces a strong dependency on the part of both parties (centralization of dependency).
2. Reciprocal-involvement creates a situation in which our commitment is contingent upon our dependency.
3. Reciprocal-involvement moderates our desire to extend commitment because of the vulnerable position in which it places us.

The three conditions for love-involvement cannot be realized in reciprocal relationships. We can, however, change a reciprocal relationship into love. It would seem to begin with coming to the realization that our strong dependency upon each other must be decentralized to some extent and that, in order to gain new sources of gratification, we will probably have to shift some of our commitment as well. Decentralized dependency as a necessary condition for love-involvement then leads to the proposition that we can't love or give unselfishly to another until we have other sources on which we can rely. Accepting this line of reasoning, those of us involved in a reciprocal relationship must paradoxically create a new contract to discontinue a contractual relationship. We must openly agree to develop involvements with others as well as each other. We must function on the principle that we *cannot really love another person until others are willing to love us.*

The above discussion illustrates another subtype of involvement which I will refer to as displacement. *Displacement-involvement can be defined as the extent to which we extend commitment to a source or sources and are dependent upon another source or other sources;* that is, the extent to which we take rewards from one place and put them in another. This kind of involvement can take on one of four general patterns:

1. Taking from one and giving to another.
2. Taking from one and giving to some others.
3. Taking from some and giving to one.
4. Taking from some and giving to some others.

Before discussing this type of involvement, I would like to consider the possibility of our being able to give continuously without taking, or, to extend our commitment without developing dependency. The assumption here is that in a personality system, there is a constant tendency to maintain a balance between the input and output of rewards. That is, when in need of gratification, we tend to concentrate on developing dependency, and when we have an abundance of rewards, we tend to extend commitments. Therefore, it would seem plausible that rewards can be accumulated and unselfish giving forthcoming. There is, however, an illusion of generosity here. There is a limit as to how much any one of us can give. As our deprivation increases, the probability that we will continue to give tends to decrease. Sooner or later our responses will shift from giving to taking. The more we are drained at any given time, the more drastic our demands will be. The supposition that we can function indefinitely without an input of rewards is as improbable as an individual functioning indefinitely with a finite supply of food.

With this in mind, our giving of rewards or commitment to another without taking from that person necessarily implies a displaced taking or dependency. In terms of the general theoretical perspective, the extension of our commitment to another person over a period of time without developing any dependency upon that person is probable only when at least one other source of gratification is available to us. Excluding the possibility of possessing an oversupply of rewards, the most tenable explanation of our generosity would seem to be that we take rewards from one place and put them somewhere else.

What this amounts to is that by satisfying another person (centralizing commitment) without expecting some return (no contingency), our love-involvement is maximized. But this increases our dependency upon others. What happens is that as we take without giving from one source (self-involvement) and give without taking to another source (love-involvement), we may well benefit the latter but may exhaust, either economically or psychologically, the former. (The previous example of the person who practices the double standard applies here.) Thus, it is possible to be committed to (or to love) only one person, but in doing so we must dependently exploit another or several others. In turn, the one to whom we are committed may be exploiting us. As our love-involvement increases in one direction, our self-involvement increases in another. The same kind of exploitation takes place in the reverse situation where we are solely dependent upon one other person and we distribute our commitment among several others.

These hardly seem like the most desirable models for interpersonal involvement since they restrict the possibilities of our *wanting* to give to those who gave to us or *wanting* to take from those who took from us. This, by the way, would not be a variation of reciprocal involvement. Reciprocity is *being expected to give* and *expecting to take* rather than wanting to give and take. Wanting to give, whether we get something in return or not, is characteristic of love-involvement. The primary criterion for giving in love-involvement is the extent to which the person receiving our rewards needs them, whether or not they have given to us or ever had any intention of giving. Thus, in practice, the displacement of involvement (centralizing commitment and decentralizing dependency or decentralizing commitment and centralizing dependency) doesn't seem to be the most love-producing alternative. Perhaps giving partly to and taking partly from a few would be more conducive to loving relationships. We would then be scattering our dependencies and commitments, but not so much that they would be superficial.

I have reviewed the arguments suggesting that self-, reciprocal-, and displacement-involvements fail to produce love. Now let's consider situations in which both commitment and dependency are more decentralized.

In Figure 5-3, I attempt to illustrate the process of developing an involvement when we are *love-oriented*. As in reciprocal-involvement patterns, we would begin the relationship with the notion of unselfish giving and receiving. Unlike reciprocal-involvement, however, we will become aware of the consequences of developing too much dependency upon the other person (convergence and its implications). By allowing our dependency to increase, we would tend to revert back to a reciprocal or even to a self-orientation. We would therefore make a concerted effort to level off our dependency and divert a part of it to other sources. Again, unlike the reciprocal pattern,

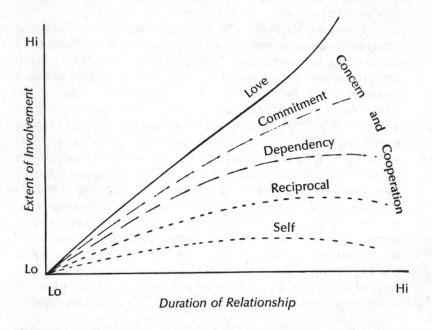

FIGURE 5-3 Love-Involvement in Developing Dyadic Relationships

we would not cut off our involvement with others. We would continue to spend time on our new relationship, perhaps quite a bit of time at first, but would be aware that as our dependency increases, we would have to reduce the amount of time spent on the new relationship and pick up on the maintenance of our older relationships—as well as keep open the possibility of an even newer one. This kind of tapering off or moderating the amount of our time spent with the new source is perhaps the first indication that our relationship will become love-oriented rather than reciprocal. The preservation of the older involvements cannot be emphasized too much. In doing this, we would not expect too many rewards from any one source and our dependency would become more decentralized—one of the necessary conditions for love as I outlined them. If the new relationship is very satisfying, moderating it can be extremely difficult. The tendency seems to be, when we are enjoying strong reward inputs ("grooving" on another person), to become satiated (spending more and more time with them). It is, appropriate here to cite a behavioristic principle. It states that the more of a particular kind of reward we receive, the less valuable any additional rewards of the same kind become. Research has also indicated that rewards administered at variable intervals seem to be more valuable than rewards at regular or continuous periods.[7] In light of this and in order to maintain maximum gratification, it would seem that in the process of developing a relationship, we would want to gain rewards from each other at irregular time periods rather than spend all of our time together. In doing this, we would tend to maximize our gratifications and also provide time during the intervals to maintain our relationships with others. Such rationality, however, is traditionally smothered by compulsive romanticism.

If our dependency is distributed among two or three or more sources, we will become more secure, less vulnerable, and less threatened. We will be in a position to shift our being rewarded or gratified from one source to another, thus making any given source less crucial in satisfying our needs. Our total dependency is not reduced, but it becomes negligible on any given source. To enable people to be more loving, our object is not to destroy dependency but to minimize its importance to any given individual at any given time. In doing this, we can divert concern for ourselves to concern about others. Because our needs are in good shape, we can think of others even if they do not reciprocate. The loss of contingency allows us to take the "you're OK even if I'm not OK" position. Our altruistic unselfishness can last as long as our own needs continue to be satisfied.[8] This, as I have argued, is largely a function of how reliable our sources are and how many sources are available.

Under the diffused dependency condition, we can afford to lose a source of gratification without greatly disrupting our functioning as a loving person. Danger occurs when several sources become less reliable or completely withdraw their commitment. If all of our sources are withdrawn in any need area, we can expect to revert to self-involvement; if all but one source is withdrawn, to a reciprocal condition.

Let's look once more at the argument which maintains that if our one available source is suddenly withdrawn, we can find another. This might be the case. The problem, of course, is our gratification during the interim period. We would have to revert to self-involvement and build it up to reciprocal-involvement. Our involvement pattern would fluctuate between self and reciprocal as our sources fluctuated between none and one. We could never, under these conditions, reach the state of being a loving person. This occurs, for example, with serial or progressive monogamy.

I am thus assuming that we are first selfish until our needs are satisfied and secured. We may then think of others. Secondly, I have argued that by decentralizing our dependency we also tend to decrease its threatening effects upon us. Thus we could maintain the maximum amount of security with the minimum amount of dependency on any given person at any given time. As our dependency becomes more secure and less a concern, our energies will tend to focus more on our giving and our commitments to others, on loving them rather than needing them.

As our dependency becomes more decentralized in love-involvement, so will our commitment. We will be able to realize that displacement is a form of exploitation and will attempt to give our commitment to the extent to which we become dependent. This is not a form of reciprocity, however. Our giving and taking would not be done on a conditional basis. Rewards would be offered and accepted primarily on the basis of need. In a love-involvement relationship, we would be able to distribute our rewards among those with whom we are involved, and it would be our task to make this evaluation and to act in a manner which would maximize their satisfaction. If one of them were in great need and the others not, we would be able to temporarily concentrate our giving to that person. If they are all equally needy, we would be able to distribute our rewards as equally as possible among them. Their needs, not ours, would determine to whom we distribute our resources.

Rewards also may be of greater value to some people than to others. A noteworthy suggestion is that the key of human exchange is to give others rewards that are more valuable to them than they are costly to us and to get from them rewards that are more valuable to us than are costly to them.[9]

Having more than one person to whom we are committed allows us to use our resources more efficiently. If only one person is dependent upon us, we may be able to give more to that person than is needed. Thus, some of our resources are wasted. On the other hand, that person might need more than we can give at that time. In the latter case, we become drained and still more is demanded. Problems arising from this kind of situation can be handled when each of us is able to turn to other sources for help. In a system based upon love-involvement, this would be possible.

In a loving relationship we do not expect a return of rewards from any person at any given time for the extension of our commitments. We may hope that others give to us when we are in need, but we would not expect rewards from any *given* person. The assumption is that if we cannot get what we need, we can try our alternate sources. Our attitude at any time would be, "If you can't satisfy my needs, I will go somewhere else to get them satisfied." I don't think this implies a resentment or bitterness. It is facing the situation and taking a realistic position. The resentment and bitterness come when our only source is not available and our relationship is possessive and reciprocal. Our needs are in demand and we are left unsatisfied. In the loving relationship, however, the response will be, "I can't satisfy you. What can I do to help you find someone else who can satisfy you?" The situation abounds in concern, not contingency; in cooperation, not competition.

If our mates, for example, are sexually frustrated and we cannot provide this kind of satisfaction at that particular time, we might respond in one of three ways. We might be completely disinterested, telling them to stop bothering us, but still demanding their total sexual fidelity. This is self-involvement. We might reluctantly concede to gratify their need, faking our own pleasure with the expectation of getting gratification in return when we have some need. This is reciprocal-involvement. Or we may encourage them to find someone else to engage sexually. To be able to respond sincerely in this manner when we are sexually dependent upon our mates to some degree indicates a love relationship. Suggesting that they find an alternative source when we are not dependent upon them for sexual satisfaction is no difficult task. To do it when we are dependent upon them is something else. Few people have reached the state of showing real love for their mates. Our lack of love in monogamous relationships is quite apparent as we threaten our mates with the dictum, "If I ever catch you with another woman (man), we're through!"

As a loving person, what would our attitude be toward the ones we love? If we are concerned about their security, we must tell them not to become too dependent upon us. If we become their sole source of gratification, we put them in a threatened position. If something happens to us, it would cause them great discomfort, in that they cannot receive from us. As a loving person, we must then encourage them to become involved with others and decentralize *their* dependencies. They may resist our encouragement and misinterpret it as our losing interest in them. We should then convince them that this is not the case and offer reassurance of our commitment to them. This can be difficult for both parties, especially during a period which is highly and mutually rewarding. If our emotions rather than our reason prevail and our dependency is not decentralized enough, we will eventually revert back to a reciprocal-involvement pattern. *It is thus to our interest, paradoxically, to be concerned with the interest of others and to encourage others not to become too interested and dependent upon us.* If our reason prevails and those whom we love attempt to establish alternate sources of gratification, they would then need our commitment less and could return our love even more.

If they are in need of excessive commitment, we could extend it to them *temporarily* until they have an opportunity to build alternate sources. After this happens, our commitment to them can be moderated. The important thing to impress upon those to whom we are committed is that, although our commitments are distributed among more than one, during periods of individual need, it would be concentrated on that individual. This general flexibility, moderation, and need-orientation in distributing commitment and rewards is a necessary condition for increasing others' security and for building reliable relationships.

To maximize general satisfaction and security, we can continually attempt to shift our dependency to those who have an oversupply of rewards and to increase our commitments to those who are more deprived. Love-involvement then consists in supplying gratification primarily when others need it, and taking gratification only when we lack it.

It is with these propositions in mind that new structures for interpersonal relations and family living may be experimented with and evolved. Perhaps, someday, we can "eat our cake and have it too," as we become more loving people.

6 ALTERNATIVE MODELS FOR INVOLVEMENT

.... And stand together, yet not too near together:
For the pillars of the temple stand apart,
And the oak and the cypress grow not
in each other's shadow:

—Kahlil Gibran, *The Prophet*

Two factors I have argued to be extremely important in describing pair attachments are the degree of our involvement and the durability of our relationship. I have shown that the extent, intensity, or strength of commitment and dependency can vary from *partial* to *total*. That is, we can be partly committed or partly dependent upon another, or we can be totally committed or totally dependent upon another. Involvement can then range from *partial* to *total* for any given individual at any given time. The durability of our relationship, on the other hand, refers to how long our involvement period is to be extended; it is a function of time. The longer our involvement period is extended, the more *permanent* the relationship. The shorter the involvement period, the more *temporary* the relationship. Using these two factors—extent and duration of involvement—I derived four possible models of interpersonal relationships: *partial-temporary, total-permanent, total-temporary,* and *partial-permanent.*

THE PARTIAL-TEMPORARY MODEL

This model implies that our relationship involves little commitment and dependency and will last for a relatively short period of time. Our relationship is somewhat superficial and provides little security for anyone involved. The limited dependency which this model allows leaves us with no reliable source of gratification. Interaction with the other person is commonly self-oriented. We are each out to see how we can profit from the transaction. Because of the lack of commitment and durability, there is little concern for the satisfaction of one another. Exploitation is most probable, and love-involvement is most uncommon.

Examples of this model include clerk-customer encounters, brief acquaintances, professional visits, short romantic affairs, orgies, or prostitution. In terms of us as individuals, it may include short part-time jobs, vacations, or temporary interests. These kinds of relationships may serve to satisfy our immediate needs but do not provide us with any kind of long-lasting security unless they are extended and transformed into one of the other models.

THE TOTAL-PERMANENT MODEL

This model is the extreme opposite of the partial-temporary. It implies that our relationship with someone involves our complete commitment and dependency and will last indefinitely. I have discussed the consequences of this kind of involvement at length in the preceding chapter. These include our centralization of involvement in one other person, or activity, or interest, thus leading us to a reciprocal kind of relationship. The ultimate effects of our using this model include a reduced sense of security; the inability to give love; increased anxiety; feelings of threat, jealousy, and possessiveness; and of course the lack of an alternative source for our satisfaction. Its highly restrictive nature provides us with little mobility, variety, or growth. In many cases, it leaves us in a rut, bored with life and generally reconciled, but unhappy.

Examples of applying this model include our having only one job, one interest, one friend, or one mate. The emphasis is on the *one*, since all our involvement is centered there. Furthermore, our one job is considered to be lifelong, our one interest is considered to last indefinitely,and we have our one mate "til death do us part." Traditional monogamy is perhaps the best example of this model. In marriage we are expected to be totally and permanently committed to one another.

The first two models best exemplify the kinds of sexual-emotional relationships which presently dominate Western society. During the courtship or uncommitted period, interaction tends to be of the *partial* and *temporary* style. Our tendency, upon meeting a new acquaintance, is to consider them either as someone to temporarily satisfy our sexual or emotional needs or, at the other extreme, as a possible marriage partner with *total* and *permanent* expectations. We rarely consider alternatives between these extremes. Even after marriage, our secondary mate relationships must be superficial due to our strong primary commitment. Marriages in which the partner or partners have secret outside lovers or mistresses (affairs) are becoming more common and perhaps more tolerable. In these cases, we function under the partial-temporary and the total-permanent models at the same time. If the marriage breaks up, we revert to the superficial partial-temporary model, until a new total commitment emerges. And the cycle begins again.

THE TOTAL-TEMPORARY MODEL

This model implies that our relationship involves complete commitment and complete dependency but will only last for a limited period of time. The advantage of this kind of relationship is that it provides us with one strong reliable source of gratification during the involvement but also allows for disinvolvement with ease and the subsequent establishment of a new relationship. The process which tends to accompany the use of this model can best be described as *serial involvement*—becoming totally involved, becoming disinvolved, and becoming totally involved again, *ad infinitum* and perhaps *ad ignorantiam*.

Examples of applying this model include our changing jobs regularly, dropping our old friends or groups when we get new ones, or the marriage-remarriage cycle (monogyny). When this model is used, the possibility of developing a permanent and secure relationship is limited. Growing, deep, and meaningful involvements are abruptly terminated as we break off our total commitments to begin again . . . and again. If our relationships are prolonged, they tend to evolve into reciprocal and contractual arrangements and would eventually move into total-permanent categories.

The trend in sexual-emotional relationships seems to be shifting from vacillation between partial-temporary and total-permanent models (superficial polygamy and traditional monogamy) to use of the total-temporary type (serial monogamy or sequential polygamy). The gradual increase of the marriage and remarriage rates over the past few decades, along with the liberalization of divorce laws, seem to be contributing to this trend. Many young couples don't even bother to get formally married; they live together under the traditional monogamous norms as long as both of them are contented with the arrangement. This is known as pair bonding. When one of them decides to end the relationship, they separate and seek out a new partner for a similar agreement. Thus, their commitment and their dependency remain centralized, total, and monogamous, but the duration of their involvement is temporary. The major problem with this sort of serial monogamy, as I see it, is the insecurity which accompanies the interim period when we "break up" with our old partners and search out new acquaintances. The major advantages of serial monogamy, on the other hand, include the possibility for variety, mobility, and growth. Possessiveness, jealousy, the inability to love, boredom, and restrictiveness are curtailed perhaps to the extent to which the duration of our relationships is limited and our involvements are less than total. Many of my other arguments against traditional monogamy still apply (see Chapter 1). Serial monogamy, nevertheless, seems to be part of our steadily emerging transient society.

THE PARTIAL-PERMANENT MODEL

This model requires some commitment and dependency, but this moderated involvement is extended for an indefinite period. Only under this model can we develop more than one meaningfully permanent relationship. Our partial commitment and dependency can be extended to two, or three, or more, other people, but in each case it can be lifelong. This model is most closely related to a love-involvement relationship. It provides us with alternative sources of gratification and the conditions for not becoming too dependent upon any one of them. It is in direct contrast with the total-temporary type in that the latter provides for no alternative sources of gratification and lasts for a relatively short time period.

Milton Mayeroff, in his discussion of "How Caring May Order Life," speaks of "appropriate others" somewhat in the manner I have described those to whom we are committed. He maintains that from a short-term point of view, an appropriate other might be a book we are writing; from a long-term point of view, certain ideas or ideals in all our writings. Thinking of appropriate others using the short-term view only implies changing appropriate others often, and not recognizing and valuing objects of continuing devotion. Also, as in this last model,

> I am "on call" for my appropriate others. This does not simply mean I am available in the sense of being open and receptive, but corresponds to the way the person "off duty" may be reached and called in when he is needed. The man who cares for his

appropriate others aspires to be always available to them when they really need him: the caring parent can be called away from something else to return to his child; the caring doctor can be reached by his patient; the caring artist is at the call of his work of art. Wherever I am, whatever I may be doing, I am subject to being called in by my appropriate others. In this sense, I may be said to be always on hand.[1]

Some examples of this model include the normal parental involvement with two or more children, having two or three permanent part-time occupations at one time, developing interests and avocations in a few areas, and having more than one mate relationship simultaneously. This model closely fits the conditions of love-involvement and may be seen as reflecting the more advanced stage of interpersonal relations. In the sexual-emotional area it would provide us with the maximum amount of growth, mobility, and love with the minimum amount of frustration, insecurity, and possessiveness. Although the potentials of this model have not been realized by the vast majority, we would expect it to become more prominent as groups, communities, and societies pass from forms of superficial involvement and traditional monogamy, through serial monogamy, to what might be termed moderated polygamy or multilateral relations.

The *partial-permanent* and *love-involvement* models could provide the conceptual foundation for interpersonal relationships in a new kind of family structure. When members of such a family would be in need, others able to give in that need area would come to their assistance, sharing a commitment to help. In a complementary sense, the members' dependencies on one another would be reliable, moderate, and collective rather than temporary and centralized.

These models for interpersonal involvement include only two important factors. For this reason they are rather simplistic in nature, especially in that each of the two variables are treated dichotomously The four models can better be seen as ideal types, recognizing that real relationships, in most cases, fall somewhere among them, but perhaps, closer to one type than to others. I view these models as theoretical constructs which we can use to aid in our understanding of interpersonal relationships and in our formation of more complex models. We must use additional factors to qualify the generalizations, to extend the theoretical relevance, and to build models which explain more and are less simplistic.

7 BEYOND THE NUCLEAR FAMILY

> All that is good and commendable now existing
> would continue to exist if all marriage laws were
> repealed tomorrow. . . . I have an inalienable
> constitutional and natural right to love whom I may,
> to love as long or as short a period as I can, to change
> that love every day if I please.
>
> —Victoria Claflin Woodhull

A world revolution is taking place in our patterns of family living. It is, first, the change in which a wide variety of family patterns in an equally wide variety of cultures throughout the world are slowly disintergrating. These traditional extended structures seem to be breaking down into smaller and smaller units. The logical consequence of this trend is the proliferation of the smallest possible unit that we can define as a family—the remnant of a broken nuclear unit—a one-parent family. The fragmentation thus reaches a dead end which sets the stage for the second kind of change. At this point, the trend is reversed as our family units grow in size. But this time the extended form takes on new and different dimensions, dimensions which are no longer founded on our old notions of marriage and kinship ties.

We can view these revolutionary family patterns as representing different stages of development. I will attempt to elaborate on some of the social and psychological forces and processes which parallel or contribute to changes at each of these stages.

STAGE I: THE CONSANGUINE FAMILY

Our traditional family system has taken on many diverse forms from one culture to another and from one time to another. However different these forms, a few social structural states seem to be characteristic of many of these families. Perhaps the most important feature of our traditional structure is the close ties among blood relatives. Our kinship-oriented extended clans are typically characterized by authoritarian role structures, exploitation of sexuality, and some kind of ascribed status for family members. Interpersonal involvements also vary from sexual promiscuity and captive marriage to highly exploitive types of matriarchy and patriarchy in some polygamous forms. Largely due to the lack of industrialization, these families are not very mobile. In their relative isolation, they develop a wide range of forms, perhaps determined by local geographic and economic conditions. They seem to evolve from a variety of conditions and at an equally diverse rate.

STAGE II: THE CONJUGAL FAMILY

With industrialization and urbanization, family forms throughout the world seem to be undergoing vast changes. William Goode suggests that these alterations have been in the direction of some type of conjugal family pattern.[1] This convergence, he argues, is toward fewer kinship ties, distant relatives, and a greater emphasis on the nuclear family unit of a couple and children. He quickly qualifies this in stating that these changes begin at different points and that each may be progressing at different rates of speed. The proliferation of this small nuclear unit is an extreme departure from the various extended family forms which have prevailed over the centuries.

The ideology of the conjugal unit is a radical one, destructive of the older traditions in almost every society. It grows from a set of more general radical principles which also arouse these groups *politically* in perhaps every under-developed country. Its appeal is almost as universal as that of "redistribution of land." It asserts the equality of individuals, as against class, caste or sex barriers.[2]

The ideology of our conjugal family gives us the right to choose our own spouse, our own kin obligations, and our own place to live. It asserts the worth of us as an individual against inherited wealth and control by our elders. It demands the independence of the nuclear family unit and relative exclusion of blood relatives from our everyday affairs. Thus, our family ties shift from an emphasis on kinship to marriage, from family lineage to a primary adjustment between spouses. Status becomes more a matter of our achievement rather than our family background, and a more egalitarian role structure provides women with the right to work and compete with their husbands.

Our interpersonal involvement patterns also change. As our dependence on affection and sexual-emotional gratification becomes centralized in our spouse (total-permanent), an unstable situation is more likely to occur and threaten the continuity of our family. Our divorce rates begin to rise, and with the liberalization of divorce laws, the rates increase even more. Remarriage is likely because there is no larger kin unit to absorb our children. The marriage-remarriage cycle continues, producing a new kind of involvement pattern. Serial monogamy or progressive polygamy become more acceptable as our marital commitments are reduced in duration from lifelong to clusters of years (total-temporary). Our relationships become contractual in nature and reciprocity the norm by which we run our everyday lives. Romantic love is our ideal, but the market economy, with its forms of exchange, competition, and property rights, sets the real model for our involvement. Competition for our mates and possession of them occur frequently during the early part of a relationship; later, we exchange mates (swapping) or change mates (remarriage). Property rights are defined primarily by our conjugal bond and having a single mate and a single set of parents is considered ideal.

Along with the ideological change, our conjugal unit is evolving in response to the demands of an increasingly industrialized world. Industry has needs which "fit" our conjugal family form. Being achievement-based, our industrial society is necessarily open-class, requiring both our geographic and our social mobility. Our industrial system requires its workers to move about freely in the labor market. Our nuclear family has this capacity to alter its residential location. Also, the function of providing emotional support to individuals complements the lack of it in the industrial system. The last argument for the fit between the conjugal unit and industrialization is that a wider variation of job roles is permitted in our nuclear form than the traditional, which in turn permits freer choice of careers as well as tolerance for training prior to marriage. In presenting these arguments, Goode is careful to note that he has not conclusively established that industrialization has caused the breakdown of the traditional extended family. Nevertheless, he does present a well-documented case for the concomitant emergence of our conjugal unit and industrialized society.

Should we then be willing to accept that as industrialization and urbanization flourish the proliferation of the nuclear family and its fragmentation will constitute the end of family change? Where is the future of the family? What forms can we expect the family to take on next, or will the family as a functioning unit of society totally disintegrate?

The trend in middle-class America seems to involve our shifting family functions to our other institutions. Schools and day-care centers are providing for more and more of the socialization of our children. Economic requirements, emotional support, and sexual gratification are becoming more a function of our individual choice and association in voluntary groups than of our family life. So, do we really need a family? Or, if a new kind of family form emerges, what will its structure and functions be like?

Perhaps the best clue as to the nature of the family of the future can be found in the most industrialized and urbanized areas of the world. Within these areas I might further narrow my focus to the young and most educated, for if any segment of society is a key to the future, this would be it. I can only extrapolate from the patterns of interpersonal relations and cooperative living which are emerging among these young-educated-urban members of society, and from these inferences develop a construct of what the trend in family structuring will be like. Such a construct will necessarily be theoretical, derived from projected trends, observations, intuitions, and perhaps too much from my biases. It will be what is known sociologically as an *ideal type*, a construct which reflects a possible objective reality and designed as a strategy in organizing relevant empirical contingencies.[3] The validity of the construct rests totally on the extent to which family patterns in the most highly industrialized and urbanized segments of the world population increasingly take on its characteristics.

As the conjugal family continues to dissolve, two possible trends seem likely. Either the functions which were traditionally performed in the family will be transferred to other agencies, such as day-care centers and encounter groups, as family life completely disappears, or new and probably diverse extended forms will come into existence to meet the demands of modern societies. Assuming that some form of family life will continue to evolve, let's look at the social forces and processes which might contribute to its emerging structures.

Industrialization and all of its ramifications can be expected to parallel the evolution of a new extended form just as it has accompanied the evolution of the conjugal unit. The new extended forms, however, will have to be structured in a manner that will more closely meet the needs of an ever-increasingly industrialized world. The forms will necessarily be designed so that we will be able to more freely move from one unit to another without threatening our family stability. This would entail a structure which has a broader base of economic support, where perhaps several adults work and contribute financially, and where the security of our family will not suffer if any of our members move to another area or family unit.

Along with pressures from industry to build a more flexible family form, increased automation will lead to a shorter and shorter work week, allowing more time for us to develop our interpersonal relationships. As industry hires greater proportions of women employees, the role of the full-time housewife will become less attractive. With more time available and more exposure to members of the opposite sex, a climate will be created where involvements outside of the conjugal relationship will become more prevalent. Extramarital sex will become more the rule than the exception. This trend will first result in the popularity of types of marriage and later, with our declining desire to marry at all. There should be, within the next decade or two, a visible decline in the rate of marriage, especially in the more highly industrialized and educated segments of the world's population.

Industrialization will then continue to accompany radical changes in family structure, but other and perhaps more important influences will allow for significant changes in our interpersonal involvements. Scientific inventions and discoveries have led to the reduction of the economic function of the family, the average age at marriage, family size, the number of family functions, and the general organization of the family itself.[4] Medical science and technology have provided measures of birth control and cures for venereal diseases, and have significantly increased our life expectancy. Medical advances in these areas are bound to have an impact on emerging forms of family life.

When our kinship and conjugal ties are considered important, who we mate with is also crucial, for it is our offspring who inherit our wealth and power. But when effective birth control is available and used extensively our mating pattern becomes less a function of procreation and lineage and more a function of whomever we feel like mating with and whenever we feel like doing it. Our mating becomes more a consequence of our immediate need and drive and less a consequence of social expectations. I suspect that a combination of the availability of birth control, the needs for affection, emotional support, and sexual satisfaction, and the de-emphasis on kinship ties will result in a morality which is more receptive to multilateral mating. Reducing the fear of pregnancy allows women as well as men to express their sexuality more openly—within or outside of any monogamous bond—and I would expect them to do just that. Thus the technology used in perfecting methods of birth control will contribute to the evolution of widespread polygamy and extraordinary sexual practices.

The other area of medical advancement which will significantly contribute to our multilateral mating is control of venereal disease. Although venereal disease is quite common, effective treatment will reduce our fear of becoming infected. I would argue that when genital infections can be treated effectively, their occurrence contributes to the breakdown of monogamous relationships. It is difficult to convince our mates of our being faithful if we contract such an infection. However, when our involvement assumes an open multilateral dimension, the transfer of venereal disease would not seem to jeopardize our relationships. The spread of these infections is partly due to our failure to inform our contacts immediately. This kind of communication will increase when our fear of rejection diminishes and when open and multiple mating relationships become more accepted. Communication breaks down when our contract is monogamous and our behavior is polygamous. Genital infections, with all their negative aspects, will have the one positive effect of making us more honest in our sexual relationships.

The technological improvement of abortion methods and their subsequent legalization will also help, both in reducing the fear of pregnancy and in providing women, once pregnant, the opportunity to not give birth to the child. It will allow women to express their sexuality more freely and to free themselves from the responsibility of motherhood. Their choice to not become a mother will then allow them greater entry into the job market and the pursuit of a career. Birth control and abortion as a form of birth control will contribute to the feminist objective of bringing about more egalitarian sex-role structures in both industry and the family. The result of placing more women outside of the home and into the market economy also increases their availability in the mating market. The probability of our finding alternative mates would seem to be partly a function of this availability. All of these results are related to the increased use of various forms of birth control.

In addition to these considerations, medical technology will continue to lengthen our life expectancy. Even if women choose to be housewives and mothers, these roles are limited to only about half of their adult lives. As children leave home, the mother is left with over a score of years to pursue new careers and new mate relationships outside of the home. Even if they do not choose employment, the great amount of time at their disposal provides them with the opportunity to become involved with other people.

These kinds of social conditions should radically change our interpersonal relations and family life style in the future. Given a situation where birth control is readily available, venereal diseases can be prevented and cured, more free time is available through automation and increased life expectancy, industry demands residential mobility, the anonymity of urbanized life veils new relationships, and education informs people about new and different mating patterns, a great deal of strain will be placed upon the no longer radical conjugal bond. The forces of industrialization, urbanization, and education which are aiding the breakdown of the consanguine family will be supplemented by medical technology, and will contribute to the breakdown of the conjugal family as well.

These are the social conditions which will probably accompany the second world revolution in family patterns and cause the emergence of communal family forms. Our ideal type communal family will be constructed primarily upon the premise that these social forces will increase as we are confronted with the future.

The evidence supporting the breakdown of conjugal ties under the social conditions which I have described is extremely sparse, and perhaps the time for evaluation is premature. The divorce rates in urbanized, industrialized, and highly affluent and educated populations, however, are on the rise. The best indication of the deterioration of marriage as an institution may be found when the number of divorces exceeds the number of marriages. For example, one of the most highly industrialized, urbanized, and highly educated areas of the country is in Santa Clara County, California. Here birth control is readily available, abortions are easy to obtain, clinics with effective treatment for venereal diseases are common, and divorce laws are liberalized. These are the preconditions for the emergence of the communal family. One of my students has just reported the current divorce rate; it is over 100 percent. There are now 101 divorces for every 100 marriages. I would expect this trend to be reflected in other areas of the world as the same kinds of social forces increase in prominence.

Numerous communal family experiments are being conducted. With this kind of experimentation and the decreasing interest in marriage as a life style, new and different family forms will become more popular. The beginning of a middle-class communal movement is now apparent and will probably gain momentum. The one-parent family where the mother works part-time, some public aid is provided for the children, and day-care facilities or baby-sitters are employed, represents the ultimate fragmentation of the nuclear system and sets the stage for the communal revolution.

The transition from the conjugal to the communal family unit begins with high divorce rate and the popularity of a marriage-remarriage cycle. As we find marriage and the nuclear family failing to satisfy our needs we begin to either live alone or live outside of wedlock with one or more spouses or friends. Census data indicate that this is already the trend in the United

States. Between 1960 and 1971 the number of individuals living alone increased about 60 percent and the number of individuals living in unrelated groups increased over 40 percent. Both of these increases are far above the general population increase.[5] The marriage rates will begin to drop significantly. As the importance of our marital ties diminish, groups of adults and children will form living units based upon friendship ties. These ties may or may not entail sexual involvement. Our sexual relationships within or outside of the communal unit will have less of an impact upon the stability of our family because our primary bond is based on friendship rather than mating patterns or kinship. Table 7-1 summarizes some characteristics of the three types of family organization.

STAGE III: THE COMMUNAL FAMILY

The emergence of the communal family begins when two unrelated adults decide to reside together and to make their situation a new life-style. As the units grow in number and different forms are experimented with, the communal structures will take on a new and different set of characteristics found in neither the consanguine nor the conjugal models.

Our communal family will increase in size to perhaps as many as 20 or 30 members, few of whom will be related as kin. By enlarging the family's size, we will create an environment where the number of our potential intimate relationships will be greatly increased, thus providing more security for each of us—especially our children who can develop long-term involvements with more than one adult of each sex. Our adult role models will not be limited to one of each sex, and continuous care for children will be guaranteed. Our children will not be left in the hands of baby-sitters of day-care centers while parents work or entertain themselves; our communal family itself will become a day-care center. Child rearing will no longer be an 18-hours-a-day job, since these duties will be shared among adults in the family unit.

TABLE 7-1 Family Typology

STRUCTURAL VARIATION	CONSANGUINE	CONJUGAL	COMMUNAL
Boundary maintenance	Kinship ties	Marriage ties	Friendship ties
Parentage	Relatives as parent substitutes	Single set of parents	Multiple parentage
Lineage	Unilateral	Bilateral	Alineal
Size of unit	Extended	Nuclear	Extended
Role structure	Sex and age distinctions	Emerging sex-role equality, age distinctions	Egalitarian age and sex roles
Power distribution	Autocratic	Oligarchic	Democratic
Social controllers	Elders	Spouses	All members
Status differentiation	Ascribed differences	Achieved differences	No status differences
Mode of wealth distribution	Inheritance	Exchange	Need
General structuring	Stable, rigid, authoritarian	Unstable, semirigid, fragmented	Stable, loose, pluralistic
Interfamily mobility	None	Limited (adoption and remarriage)	Commonplace

Mate involvement	Polygyny-polyandry (partial-temporary)	Monogamy (total-permanent)	Serial monogamy (total-temporary)	Polygamy (partial-permanent)
Involvement pattern	Self-involvement (highly decentralized)		Reciprocal-involvement (highly centralized)	Love-involvement (somewhat decentralized)
Emotional emphasis	Pride, restraint, fear, shame, frustration		Jealous love, passion, guilt, resentment	Empathetic love, compassion, joy
Value emphasis	Collectivism-materialism (biological determinism)		Individualism-existentialism (self-determinism)	Humanism-scientism (social determinism)
Personality structure	Parent-superego dominance (prescriptive)		Child-id dominance (inscriptive)	Adult-ego dominance (descriptive)
Social processes	Coercion-conflict		Contract-competition	Concern-cooperation

The ages of our family's members will range from very young to elderly. By always having some children in our unit, we will be able to assume parental roles when and for as long as we want. Children will also be exposed to teenage parent figures. Older members of our family, who would be treated as part-time baby-sitters in the conjugal unit, will participate as fully in child-rearing duties as any of the other adults—perhaps even more as they retire from their careers and have more free time. In this way our communal family will provide a major function for the elderly, rather than their being isolated without much respect, responsibility, and authority. The age range will therefore provide an ongoing situation in which various age groups continuously participate in family activities. Because of this, it will be possible for us to be born into the unit, live our whole lives, and die there—although this will not normally be the case. Such continuity in the structure will increase stability and security for the members over generations.

Our communal family, being representative of the total population of the country, will be composed of approximately three or four adults to every child. This ratio will allow for better supervision of our children and, since as parents we share children with other parents, there will be less chance of the inculcation of biased values and motives due to narrow exposure to only one or two parent figures. Our children will also have an advantage that they don't have in the nuclear family. From the adults they can select their own parents, brothers, sisters, friends, and perhaps eventually mates. Since whom we relate to will be more a function of our common interests and companionship rather than genetics, our social ties will not be forced nor strained by the mandates of kinship and marital obligations.

Close interpersonal identifications in our communal family will be expected to last only as long as both parties desire to continue them. As a result of these kinds of attachments, we will not take one another for granted. We will have to strive continuously to nuture our relationships with others, since the duration of these relationships will not be legally or morally contrived nor sanctioned. There will be an absence of any family norm forcing us to continuously relate closely to any particular other member. Mutual concern and enjoyment will be the determining factors which will prolong any of our involvements.

Responsibility to others will be diffused and rotated and will therefore be more open-ended. One of the most impressive effects of our larger communal structure will be the possibility of alternatives in interpersonal relations. This is not possible in the conjugal family, primarily because of its smaller size.

In breaking down our kinship and marital ties, control over the young by the old using economic sanctions and inheritance will be eliminated. Agism as well as sexism will become things of the past. Since each child will be economically independent of any adult in the family, and since inheritance will usually be given to the family at large, adult coercion will be minimized. Each of our children will be economically dependent upon adults, but the dependency will be so decentralized that intimidation using material sanctions will be all but impossible. Using the same logic, control of our mating by anyone else will be equally impossible.

One other effect of breaking down the kinship structure will be that our friendships will no longer take second place to the obligations and respect demanded for blood relatives in the older family forms. Friendship will take the place of kinship. This, of course, does not mean that friendships will not develop among the kin, only that the foundation for involvement will not be predicated upon a consanguine or conjugal premise. Love and care in our communal family will be a function of individual choice, not of socially or morally imposed expectations. The only expectation in our communal family will be that we become loving and caring people and that we will try to love and care for several others, regardless of age, sex, or the type of relationship. To whom we direct our concern and affections will not be a matter of family policy. Incest taboos will lose their potency.

The role structure in our communal family will provide several advantages over the conjugal form. By not designing roles according to sex differences, women will be able to participate equally with men in occupational ventures outside of the family and men will participate equally with women in terms of family duties and responsibilities. In identifying with all family roles, we can double our human potential, increase cross-sex empathy, and promote an intimacy which would be difficult under a differentiated sex-role structure.

Women will no longer be left in isolation to gratify their needs through fantasy, an overdependence on their children, and a materialistic outlook. They will be able to participate as fully as men in all aspects of social life. Men will also develop a much stronger father-child bond due primarily to their more equal participation in child-rearing functions.

Our children along with women will no longer have a minority status. As soon as our children are physically able and choose to contribute to family functioning they will be allowed to take on any of the roles traditionally attributed only to adults. Full rights and duties will be delegated to our children as early as possible. Control of children's behavior will not be differentiated from the kind of control one adult will enact toward another. In all cases, our sanctions will be mild and positive but carefully and systematically derived. The overall effect of eliminating sex and age differences will be the promotion of cooperation, cohesiveness, and concern among our family members.

This egalitarian structure will be reflected in our family decision-making process. An authoritarian form where elders or parents act as an oligarchy will give way to a democratic structure in which each of us, including children, will have one vote. As a dissenting member we will be given a great deal of consideration, and decisions will be worked out so that a consensus can be achieved. Our communal family will not be based upon a system of ascribed or achieved statuses. Each of us and any position we hold will be considered equally important, and the mode of distributing rewards will be done systematically according to our need rather than according to rights of inheritance or exchange.

With the abolition of monogamy the stability of our communal family will not depend upon the compatibility of two parents (as in the conjugal form), or for that matter, on the compatibility of any two people. If for any reason we feel dissatisfied with others, we will be able to move out of the family unit without disrupting its normal functioning. The stability of our family will thus not be threatened by any one person. If we leave permanently, a new member would be recruited or be born into the family to take our place. If we are called away to meet temporary occupational demands, to take a vacation, to fulfill military obligations, or for whatever reason, our family continuity will be maintained. This continuity is not so easily maintained in the conjugal unit when either the mother or father is away for any length of time. Extended illness in the nuclear family also places great strains on the remaining members. But in our communal family, the responsibility in caring for the ill will be diffused so as not to place any strain on our family. Normal day-to-day functioning will therefore seldom be disrupted.

The high rate of residential mobility so common in the nuclear family system loosens support provided by other primary groups, limits our security and companionship, and requires us to make a variety of adjustments. Our communal family, on the other hand, will not be so mobile in its location, and thus problems of adjusting to new environments will be less crucial. As we move to another family, adjustment difficulties may occur, but our family as a unit will remain stable in its location, and adjustments will be made only as individuals move in and out. The stability of the conjugal unit is also a function of the couple's isolation from competing primary loyalties. Rather than isolating couples from other social contacts to preserve their marriages, our communal norms will maintain that marriages should not be preserved, since isolating us from one another reduces our security. The loneliness and despair so common in the nuclear family, especially of the middle-aged housewife, will be virtually nonexistent in our communal family.

Our communal family will realize several advantages in eliminating the norms favoring monogamy. Total sexual-emotional involvement between two people will be modified to partial involvement among a few. This pattern will prevent both our restricted gratification and our overdependence on one person. In allowing for alternative sources of satisfaction to be readily available, our sexual-emotional security will be maximized. The overdependency found in monogamy—leading to possessive and jealous feelings—will evolve into a sharing, empathetic, and cooperative involvement in our communal setting.

Our involvement will not be characterized by a monotonous day-to-day living together as is so common among conjugal couples where discriminatory rights and duties are imposed upon each member. Rather our relationship will become more free and spontaneous, where our trusting one another takes the place of *pretending* to trust one another. It will be a kind of relationship where we will be more open because we will be less threatened and more secure, where our loving commitment will not be contingent upon our getting something in return. But above all, it will imply a free and flexible approach in our mate selection where whom we are involved with and the length of time we stay involved will be more a matter of decision between or among us, not a concern of moral or legal restrictions.

The value system in our communal family will stem from different kinds of assumptions concerning human nature. The instinctive origin of our behavior as well as the notion of our individual will and responsibility will give way to the idea that our behavior, attitudes, and feelings are largely a function of the kind of environment in which we were socialized. Truth will be seen as paradoxical in nature. The individual and the collectivity will be merged. Conflict and competition will yield to relations of cooperation, and jealous possessiveness will evolve into a loving concern. The value structure (morality and philosophy) that goes along with the communal stage will be elaborated in Chapter 11.

This then is my projected direction of change in world family patterning. The extent to which it will be realized is not a function of faith nor reason but rather of future empirical regularities. I can hypothesize and predict what will come but only history can substantiate it. To the extent to which family patterns evolve in other directions, I confess, my biases have truly gotten the best of me.

PART TWO

NEW MODELS
IN FAMILY THEORY

This part of the book is designed for the person having more theoretical and philosophical interests. It includes four new models related to different areas of thought in interpersonal relations and family forms. In Chapter 8, literature concerning love is reviewed, and the concept of love as a social psychological process is developed. In Chapter 9, a new approach to understanding our emotions is outlined. Emotions, seen as the effects of social situations, are defined and altered by these social conditions and our behavior. The last two chapters utilize the Hegelian dialectic and elaborate a conflict model of psychological gratification. The conflict model is presented in Chapter 10 as an analogue of the Marxian dialectic. This discussion begins with the countercultural rebellion against materialism and ends, in Chapter 11, with the final synthesis—a futuristic value system and a new morality.

8 LOVE AS A SOCIAL PROCESS

Perhaps we need to look more seriously at our ideas
of love and the distortions and caricatures of
love manifested around us and by us today.

—Jean Bolton

Narrow definitions of love have been abundantly offered in
literature. It has been defined as a strong emotional attachment,
as a condition in which the other person's satisfaction and
security are supreme, as empathy with our loved one, as the
optimum development of both, as being motivated by self-
gratification, as *not* being motivated by self-gratification, as a
tendency to aid our loved one, and as a caring activity rather
than a passion. Other definitions include the more romantic
and courtly elements such as the idealization of our partner, and
the importance of physical attraction, overdependency,
jealousy, and possessiveness.

Although some authorities have attempted to view love as
a multidimensional phenomenon or have attempted to de-
lineate different kinds of love, we have failed to treat the preconditions to love systematically. The disruptive effects of love
on kinship ties and stratification and the need-gratifying effects
of romantic love have been argued, but we have seen or heard
little about its social causes. I will attempt to defend the position

that loving people exist because they have been exposed to a loving environment. We love under certain conditions and not under others. In making this assumption, it is my intent to understand and conceptually reproduce the conditions which tend to maximize loving.

Many of the factors we have used in defining love can be seen, not as love itself, but as prerequisites for loving. The process of loving concerns not only emotions, predispositions, need-gratification, empathy, growth, and love activity but also, and perhaps more importantly, the kinds of environments which facilitate it. It is these social conditions which affect individuals and make them into loving or nonloving people that I will focus on in this chapter. If these conditions are adequately recreated and built into a new family system, I believe loving activity and loving feelings can be greatly increased.

LOVE AND CONCERN FOR SELF

The process of loving begins with ourselves. This does not refer to the extent to which we love ourselves but the extent to which we are loved by those around us, the extent to which we exist in an environment that promotes our self-awareness, self-gratification, and self-security. The assumption here is that before we can be loving, we have to be adequately cared for ourselves. We have to be taught to become aware of our own real needs and how to have them satisfied when they are neglected. We have to be exposed to the kind of environment which provides us with security in each of our need areas. As a loving individual we are but a reflection of our loving environment.

Step 1: Self-Awareness

Perhaps the first step in becoming a loving person is to develop our ability to recognize when one of our needs is not satisfied. This is, in effect, learning to understanding ourselves and what

we are striving for. The failure to understand or properly interpret our needs and to subsequently misdirect our behavior
circumventing their gratification results in what Snell and Gail
Putney refer to as *normal neurosis.*[1] They maintain that faulty
interpretation may include being conditioned to satisfy a need
in only one way. One form of particularization which I discussed
in earlier chapters is the centralization of dependency (for
gratification in a certain need area) in just one other source.
When we rely totally upon *that* one source for gratification, and
that source fails us, we in our neurotic unawareness are likely to
misdirect our behavior. We see our frustration, not in terms of
our source failing, but as something else being wrong. Our
behavior is thus motivated by a deprived need, but is inappro-
priate to its satisfaction. If, on the other hand, we learn to
become aware of our needs when they are frustrated, and learn
how to satisfy them, our neurosis decreases and our happiness
increases. But how is this awareness, this consciousness of self,
learned?

Being aware of ourselves is first being aware of humanity.
Being aware of our self-needs is being aware of universal human
needs, not culturally imposed felt-needs. It is being aware of
those needs which are characteristic of the species, not of a
particular social order. These universal needs involve
economic, social, and psychological rewards. They are
economic in the sense of maintaining physical conditions that
provide our body with oxygen, tolerable temperature, water,
sleep, nourishment, movement, and mental and sexual activity.
They are social in the sense of our requiring association with,
acceptance by, and a feeling of belonging to other individuals,
groups, institutions, and communities, and in a greater sense,
to the human race. Psychologically, we need to feel like a
worthy and lovable human being; we need to appreciate ourselves, to have a positive image of ourselves, and to love ourselves. The "higher" need includes self-actualization or self-
realization by which we seek purposeful activity as a means of
experiencing, exploring, and expanding our capacities.[2]

The kind of environment that allows us to become more

aware of these needs is one where we receive continuous feedback about our behavior. Self-awareness is not a function of how much we believe we are aware of ourselves nearly as much as how willing we are to see ourselves based upon the feedback we receive from people around us. A realistic self-concept is therefore formulated through our interaction with others. Although our ideal concept of ourselves (what we like to think we are) may vary from the kind of feedback we receive, this discrepancy can be a basis for growing. Not completely accepting ourselves as others see us provides us with motivation to alter our actions more in the direction of how we would like to be. Through continuous feedback from others, we can constantly check the discrepancy between our real and our ideal self-concepts. Increased feedback in the direction of our ideal self-concept can then be considered an indication of our growth.

Step 2: Self-Gratification

Once we become aware of our deficiencies and are aware that we are dependent upon our environment for removing them, we may become motivated to behave in a manner which will lead us into a more gratifying social situation. Failing to receive gratification for a frustrated need means we are distracted from loving others and become preoccupied with our own demands. The assumption that I am making here is that before we can love others we must be exposed to an environment in which we are loved by others. Before we can give, we must have gotten. Our psychological health comes from being loved, from being gratified when frustrated, rather than from being deprived of love.

> . . . society is based on love, in fact *is* but a developed form of love. . . . where hatreds exist in any person within any society we may be sure that they, too, are due to love, for hatred is love frustrated.[3]

One prerequisite for our being a loving person is then a state of not being in need.

Step 3: Self-Security

Because we have our needs gratified at a given time does not mean that we are secure. Our security, as I discussed earlier, is a function of how many reliable sources of gratification we have in each need area. When only one other person provides an abundance of affectional, erotic, or emotional gratification, an overdependency on that person may develop. If this happens, we tend to substitute a felt-need demanding the constant presence of the other for affectional and emotional rewards. We come to believe that we need the person, the *source* of gratification, rather than the gratification itself, independent of who offers it. In allowing satisfaction to originate from only that one person, we confuse the person with the reward. The extreme of this occurs in so-called romantic love. We develop a craving for complete fusion, for union with the other person. Our strong need for gratification which "only the other person can provide" becomes synonymous with our giving gratification. Our loving someone else and our needing someone else become indistinguishable. Our mutual dependency becomes so extreme that no distinction is made as to who is giving to, or taking from, whom. This kind of situation, of course, destroys any individuality we might have. We become one; that is, we come to compromise our interests, our traits, our beliefs, and our actions so as to maintain the constant company of the other. The pitfalls of reciprocal-involvement enter in. As I have argued earlier, love does not grow out of this involvement pattern. A social system reinforcing complete fusion of two people has the negative effect of curtailing the process of loving.

Erotic or romantic love, inasmuch as it involves a craving for union with one other person, is by nature exclusive, not universal; it distorts the very meaning of the word "love." We popularly equate love and need to the extent to which some authorities speak of love in contradictory terms: first in terms of centralizing commitment in one person and then in terms of decentralizing it.

> Love should be essentially an act of will, of decision to commit my life completely to that of one other person. (erotic love) [However,] If a person loves only one other person and is indifferent to the rest of his fellow men, his love is not love but a symbiotic attachment, or an enlarged egotism. (brotherly love)[4]

To define even two different kinds of love in such opposite terms is but to confuse the meaning of the word.

The notions of being in love, of courtly love, and of romantic love, are delusions of love, not love itself. They do not provide self-security but rather limit it. The concentration of involvement with just one other person allows us no other people to turn to when we are in need. The alternative to the *complete union* or *oneness* model of total and permanent involvement might be referred to as an *overlap* model in which we do not have to compromise our individuality. We share certain personality and behavioral traits with each of several other people. We are a composite of all of them rather than a duplicate of one. Being a composite of a unique aggregate of others, we maintain our own uniqueness.

A precondition to becoming a loving person, to being secure in ourselves, is thus not being *out of love* but *in love* with more than one other person; that is, having more than one need-source to depend upon. However, being in love with a few other people does not automatically make us a loving person; it again is only one of several prerequisite steps, one of the necessary conditions.

LOVE AND CONCERN FOR OTHERS

Love of ourselves becomes unnecessary and fades as love by others takes its place. Self-love decreases as self-acceptance, self-gratification, and self-security emerge. Once we become aware of our need-deficiencies, are motivated to care for them and can gratify them, and have reliable alternative sources for gratification, we are ready to start being concerned about others. We are then in a position in which our own needs are met, our own ego is not threatened, and we can afford to give without the fear of not getting something in return. We can become more removed from our inner state, from our own feelings and prejudices, and direct our attention and our rewards to others. This is the process of moving from the subjective to the objective, from the "in here" to the "out there," from narcissism to altruism—from me to you.

We thus become oriented to others, not because we desire to or will it, but because we have been motivated by an environment which has provided us with security and has reinforced in us a concern for others. At this point we have more of a potential of becoming a loving person than before, but there are still other conditions which must be met.

Step 4: Acceptance of Others

Loving other people assumes an acceptance of them. It does not necessarily mean that we completely agree with them nor that we condone the others' behavior. Acceptance involves only our assuring them that they will not be deprived of gratification if they are completely open and reveal their private feelings, thoughts, and behaviors to us. For they will probably reveal only those parts of themselves which they believe will bring them gratification. To believe them, to know them, to trust them is then a function of how sure they are that they will not suffer. Threats of coercion, rejection, or degradation on our part do not indicate acceptance. They only increase the others' defensiveness, lying, and a tendancy not to reveal private thoughts.

Our acceptance of another person can occur to different degrees for different thoughts, feelings, or actions. We can accept one behavior, but not another; one thought, but not another—and to a different degree in each case. In a marriage situation, for example, there are varying degrees to which we can accept our spouse's becoming erotically involved with another person. There are at least six levels at which acceptance of this sort takes place; they range from least acceptance to most acceptance.

1. *Destructive.* "If I ever catch you with another woman (man), I'll kill you!"
2. *Disinvolvement.* "If I ever catch you with another woman (man), our relationship is finished!"
3. *Reciprocal.* "If you hurt me by being with another woman (man), I'll do the same thing to you!" (What is good for the goose is good for the gander.)
4. *Self-protective.* "If you want to hurt me by seeing someone else, that's OK—just don't tell me about it!"
5. *Self-acceptive.* "If you would like to get involved with someone else, it's OK, so let's talk about it!"
6. *Empathetic.* "I want you to be involved with others so that you will become more secure."

We grow in terms of our accepting others as we move to the last of these levels. As we become more secure in ourselves and less threatened by, and less solely dependent upon, our loved one, we become a more accepting kind of person. Our self-concern evolves into concern for others—and, of course, our concern for and acceptance of others allow them to more fully accept us.

Our complete acceptance of others is then a state that takes place only to the extent to which the other person poses no threat to us. This happens only under two conditions: either the other person cannot be used as a source of our gratification or we have alternative sources available. The first condition implies no dependency and the second implies a diffused dependency. It is relatively easy for us to accept someone with whom we are not involved and therefore not dependent upon (such as strangers in an encounter group) or someone whom we are partly dependent upon. When total dependency on another person occurs, however, our acceptance of the other person in a given need area is difficult, if not impossible.

Step 5: Empathy

Acceptance of the other person for whatever they are or whatever they do is necessary if honest feedback from them is desired. Since others will "open up" to the extent to which they do not feel a threat of reprisal from us, successful empathy becomes a direct function of our accepting them. With total acceptance of the other person, our distorted or misconceived empathy is reduced. Honest communication between two people is a result of such mutual acceptance.

A precondition for empathy involves the casting out of our own ego so that our full concentration can be given to the other person. It is the process of making ourselves empty, of self-transcendence, of identifying with the other person so that we can understand and share the other's aims and desires.

The process of empathy, however, does not imply the negation of our inner reality, only its temporary abandonment. We lose our own feelings, thoughts, and actions but gain those of the other. The other person's objective feedback becomes for the time being the focus of formulating our new inner state, assumed to resemble the other's inner state. The process negates neither the inner subjective reality nor the outer objective reality. It involves flowing from the evacuated "in here" through the "out there" media for the purpose of acquiring information about the subjective state of another person ("in there"). It then proceeds by bringing the "in there" information through the "out there" media back into the "in here." It is a process of fusing our subjective and objective realities by losing our own "in here" so that another person's "in here" can temporarily become our own "in here."

> To care for another person, I must be able to understand him and his world as if I were inside it. I must be able to see, as it were, with his eyes what his world is like to him and how he sees

himself. Instead of merely looking at him in a detached way from outside, as if he were a specimen, I must be able to be *with* him in his world, "going" into his world in order to sense from "inside" what life is like for him, what he is striving to be, and what he requires to grow.[5]

Empathy seems to be related to projection in that they both involve the symbolic displacement of parts of ourselves. The difference is that in projection we place parts of ourselves in the other person, whereas in empathy we place parts of the other in ourselves. Both processes may be positive in that we may project onto others acceptable parts of ourselves or we may bring back to ourselves those parts of others which are considered acceptable only to ourselves. They both may be negative in that we may project undesirable parts of ourselves onto others or bring back to ourselves someone else's traits that we consider undesirable. Empathy, whether positive or negative, seems to reduce alienation from both ourselves and others while projection, whether positive or negative, seems to lead to self-alienation and alienation from others. Positive empathy is relatively easy to achieve. Negative empathy tends to facilitate growth more in that it enables us to learn to accept in ourselves those traits that we cannot accept in others. Self-criticism and humility are learned through this process. Positive empathy is also growth producing, especially if we tend to reject desirable parts of ourselves. Instead of projecting these acceptable parts onto others, we "reown" them (develop a positive self-image). Confidence and self-esteem are learned by us this way. By using both positive and negative empathy, we learn to see ourselves more realistically as having both favorable and unfavorable qualities. We learn both humility and self-appreciation, the ability to criticize ourselves but still like ourselves, to accept the notion that it is alright to not be *all* right. Empathy, as a projection reversal process, is most instructive in developing a more realistic self-concept and in our preparation for loving others.

The overall process of empathy then includes many of the

conditions for becoming a loving person. It might be summarized in the following manner:

1. *Developing an objective consciousness.* This involves the loss of our ego through self-awareness, self-gratification, and self-security.
2. *Comprehending the subjective state of the other.* This is achieved through communicating total acceptance of others, breaking down their defensiveness, and encouraging them to provide relevant information about their inner self.
3. *Symbolically recreating the subjective state of the other in ourselves.* This concerns the assimilation of information so that we can temporarily be redesigned to resemble the other's self.

Thus the kind of relationship which is most conducive to our becoming a loving person can be characterized by a sort of transparency where our real feelings are evident, by an acceptance of others as individuals with value in their own right, and by a deep empathetic understanding which enables us to see others' private worlds through their eyes. Empathy then is a necessary condition for our effective loving.

Learning to become an empathetic person is not an easy task. We do not develop this ability in the course of our everyday life. In fact, our society teaches us *not* to be concerned with the welfare of others. We are taught to be self-concerned, competitive, individualistic, and introspective. To overcome these deficiencies, I have tried an exercise in some of my classes designed to teach the students how to empathize with one another. They are divided into small groups of 6 to 8 students and the purposes of the exercise are listed:

1. To get to know how other members of the group feel within themselves about things which affect them emotionally.
2. To become so involved in understanding other mem-

bers of the group that we completely forget about asserting our own egos.

3. To so thoroughly lose ourselves in another human being that we have no desire to evaluate and criticize them.
4. To put ourselves symbolically in someone else's place so as to imagine that we are in fact them and can feel and respond as they do.
5. To temporarily become someone else.

After becoming familiar with these purposes, the students are instructed to remove their shoes, sit in a tight circle on the floor, and refrain from talking unless so instructed. As a warm-up they put their feet in the center of the circle and rub on each other's feet. The same is then done with their hands. They then look directly into the eyes of the person across the circle from them and concentrate on how that other person must feel at the moment. After a short interval, I ask them, "Can you forget yourself? Can you stop yourself from evaluating them? Do you have any idea how they must feel right now?" I then suggest, "Look at their eyes very carefully, their other facial features, the position of their bodies. Do these things tell you anything about the way they feel? Try to duplicate those feelings in yourself. Can you feel the way they do? Can you stop thinking about yourself and totally concentrate on them? Try hard to become them and feel as they must feel!" After a few minutes of this activity, I ask them to sit back, relax, and discuss informally with each other how this short exercise made them feel and the extent to which they were able to put themselves in the place of someone else. They usually find that their ability to do this is quite limited.

The second part of the exercise involves having one of the members of the group become the subject. (I have the group select the first subject on the basis of who in the group they think is best able to express feelings verbally.) The subjects lie on their backs in the center of the group. Each of the other members touches some part of the subjects' bodies with both hands during the remainder of the exercise and keeps direct eye contact. The exercise begins with members of the group asking the subjects questions about how they feel in a number of situations such as "What makes you happy? What makes you sad, or jealous, or guilty?" The questions are asked so that the subjects can communicate their important feelings to the group. The subjects try to communicate their emotions or feelings and to intellectualize their ideas or thoughts. The other members of the group are instructed to try to forget about themselves and not to evaluate the subjects. They try to put themselves in the subjects' place and try to create the feeling in themselves which they perceive in the subjects. They only ask questions and do not respond verbally in any manner to the subjects' comments.

After about ten minutes the group is asked to stop. The subjects then ask the group the same questions and the group members attempt to respond as the subjects would. This is role reversing and it provides some feedback for the group as to whether or not they were successfully empathizing. After a few minutes of feedback the members discuss why they had trouble empathizing with the subjects. Variations of this exercise can be derived and applied in teaching empathy.

But is our empathy with just one other person sufficient? If it is not possible to understand ourselves without a generalized picture of how others see us, perhaps it is also as difficult to empathize with one other person unless we have a generalized empathy. It seems to me that generalized empathy is growth producing in that it promotes our understanding of different kinds of people. However, centralized empathy, where we have concern for only one other person, is growth reducing and results in a very one-sided understanding, just as in the research process, any sample of one person yields the most biased estimate of people in a given population. Others who are like us reinforce our biases; they are easy to empathize with.

In teaching empathy using the process described above, a more generalized empathy can be achieved by letting each member of the group take turns being the subject. I have found that is easier for males to empathize with males and females with females, blacks with blacks and whites with whites, young with young and old with old, and so on. Groups which are mixed in terms of age, sex, race, and any other characteristic related to individual differences, expand our empathy. Growth implies the understanding of people who are different from us, of people who have different feelings, thoughts, and actions. We can achieve an understanding of these differences most effectively through empathy with a representative sample of all human beings, not with just one individual. This is most idealistic, but in a more practical sense, empathy with different kinds of people is possible.

The romantic model of love tends to work against empathizing with different kinds of people as the notion of oneness encourages our centralized empathy and involvement. Reciprocal patterns become dominant as convergence, disillusionment, and their consequences leave us with the illusion of oneness. Our mutual understanding and empathy are destroyed as we become overdependent, fearful of rejection, and self-defensive. We falsely believe that we are empathetic and loving as we mold and shape our partners into our own image. As our prejudices, feelings, and desires become more alike, our empathetic ability becomes inactive. Narcissism replaces understanding, for to love only someone who has been made to be so much like ourselves is to really love only ourselves, and to empathize with the other is to empathize with ourselves —which is not to empathize at all.

In order to develop our empathetic potentials, empathy must be extended to as many different kinds of people as possible. The goal must be to understand people in general, not just one person; mankind rather than a single human. Paradoxically, in order to effectively empathize with one person, we must first empathize with humanity. As we learn to put ourselves symbolically in the place of others, we expand our identifications, our biases, and ourselves. If we can empathize with people who are extremely different from us, we can empathize with anyone —and with everyone. As a loving person we must develop this capacity.

There are many factors which separate us and make empathy more difficult. I have suggested that empathy between males and females in our society is difficult. This is because of the traditional differences between the roles of the sexes. Males and females have been socialized in two distinct subcultures, each having its own language, behaviors, and values. Empathy between people of different social classes and statuses is also difficult due largely to the demand for social isolation within classes as well as the mystique surrounding the superiority of the upper strata. The social distance produced in these hierarchies gives rise to a unilateral rather than a mutual respect among us. In the family, in industry, and at school, the authority vested in some and not in others strains child-parent, owner-employee, and student-teacher relations, and makes empathy along these lines unattainable. Empathy with people who have been raised in other countries is also difficult to learn. However, as people from various cultures interact with us more, as communication becomes more effective, and as international mobility increases, a generalized universal empathy would seem to grow and flourish.

It is apparent that whenever we construct status distinctions, whether based on age, sex, race, occupation, income, or nationality, our empathy is blocked. To the extent to which somebody or some position in the social system is considered to be more important than somebody else or some other position, we cannot expect effective communication, mutual acceptance, dropping of defenses, a loss of ego-threat, increased security, and widespread gratification. A generalized empathy can be realized to the degree to which all of us and every position we fill is unique, indispensable, and important in our or its own right. Our effective empathy involves understanding differences in function, not differences in status or rank; differences in the kinds of things we do, not in their relative importance. In order to maximize our general empathy (and love), status or ranking systems must be abolished. There can be no minority status for our children, women, racial minorities, the elderly, or certain occupations or nationalities. Empathy involves our dropping our defenses and opening up to one another. We will not do this when we feel threatened by our "betters" or when we condescend to others in lower status positions.

I can think of nothing more destructive to effective empathy than status distinctions between two individuals. For example, before I can participate in empathy exercises in my classes, I have to break down the fear which students have of teachers who use power and status for evaluation. By dressing more like them, asking to be referred to by my first name, and setting up a grading system which will not penalize them for "telling me off" if they so desire, I have broken down some of the barriers—not all of them, but our deeply embedded hierarchies are difficult to destroy even at an individual level. (Most of what I have learned since I have started teaching, I have learned from my students. Strange that I should be called the teacher.) But if I can to some degree become a student, at least symbolically, my empathy for them and theirs for me will be magnified. This kind of breakdown in such relationships can be a growing experience for all of us.

Empathy also becomes extremely important in the process of loving in that it helps us to prevent faulty interpretation of our loved one's needs. If we misinterpret needs, many rewards can be wasted while those we love continue to be frustrated. The major function of empathy is then to maintain economy by discovering where and how many rewards are required for others, and to prevent their overuse or underuse. For us to overreward one person when another is in need not only adds to the waste but also diminishes the general satisfaction of everyone.

Step 6: Security of Others

When we are secure in our own needs and have learned how to accept and empathize with others, we are ready to direct our attention and concern to their needs. When the satisfaction or the security of another person becomes as significant to us as our own satisfaction or security, then the process of loving comes closer to completion.

Our concern for another's security is identical in nature to the concern we have for our own security. This includes using our empathy to discover the other person's deprived need areas. Second, it involves our desire to obtain immediate satisfaction for the other person, and finally, it is our desire to provide them with reliable alternate sources of gratification for more long-term stability and security.

THE ACT OF LOVING

The process of loving up to this point implies no behavior directed toward our loved one. It deals only with our self-gratification and our predispositions to act toward others. The act of loving, however, includes not only the actual gratification of another person but also the feeling which accompanies it and the self-satisfaction which results from it.

Step 7: Love Behavior

Love has been defined in terms of the act of giving gratification to another person. Erich Fromm in his notion of productive love, for example, insists that "love is an activity and not a passion."[6] The essence of love is to "labor" for something. The process of loving then includes an act toward the other person—not just any act, but one based upon our evaluation of the other's needs, an act designed to increase others' satisfaction where it is most deprived. We as loving people, through the empathy process, then must make a decision about how we can act so as to provide the greatest amount of gratification with the least amount of wasted time, effort, and rewards. The more efficient we are in giving gratification, the more loving we can be.

Sometimes the kind of reward people want or think they need is not what they in fact need. It is possible for us to be more aware of others' needs than they are themselves. It is quite common for those in need to be deprived to the extent to which they are unable to view themselves from an objective perspective. They may, for example, desire some behavior from us that would damage their health or reinforce some self-destructive activity. Supporting masochistic tendencies can in no way be interpreted as loving. Those who enjoy being hurt or enjoy hurting others should be viewed as being extremely deprived in certain need areas. Our response to these kinds of people should be positive and strong—but never immediately following their self-destructive or aggressive acts. People in these states have, in the past, been given attentive rewards following these acts. They have thus learned to enjoy sadomasochistic behavior. This kind of conditioning could better be defined as producing self-hate and hate for others—the complete opposite of learning to become loving people. Our positive responses that directly gratify another's needs are the most desirable, but careful attention must be paid to make sure that these responses do not directly follow, and thereby reinforce, others' masochistic or sadistic behavior.

One of our major goals in becoming a loving person is then to minimize others' self-destructive or aggressive actions and to promote a system of positive exchange. Sometimes the people being loved do not interpret our loving behavior as being what they desire, but our decision of how to act toward others must take into account awareness, acceptance, empathy, need, and security—not only what the loved ones *think* they need. Love is not giving people what they want; it is giving them what they need. They sometimes want things they don't need, want more than they need, or want support for their biases. Loving involves none of these; it is directed toward motivating growth, not stagnation, sadomasochism, overconsumption, or waste.

Step 8: The Feeling of Love

Our feeling of love is not the same as our feeling of being "in love." Being in love involves our feelings of wanting to get closer, to come in more intimate contact, to touch and embrace our loved ones, to yearn for them. This kind of euphoric feeling is the result of our overdependency on the gratification we receive from another, not because we give others rewards. Being "in love" then is not a result of our giving, but of our taking. It is, in fact, our feeling of self-need-gratification, not our feeling of love for another person. Such gratification may be the result of another's love but it has nothing to do with the feelings which are aroused in us as a loving person.

The feelings which a loving person experiences come out of empathetically gratifying others' needs. When we put ourselves symbolically in the place of another, our rewarding the other person is like rewarding ourselves. The self-satisfaction we derive from this process is the *loving feeling*. This feeling can be described as resulting from our symbolic self-gratification, from being gratified as we gratify others. Only under these conditions is it realistically possible for us to provide satisfaction for ourselves. The paradox in this case is that we can only satisfy ourselves by satisfying others. Self-love, in a healthy sense, is the by-product of the process of loving another. Because we as a loving person have symbolically received as well as given, and we have received the rewards which are mutually needed, we can symbolically define ourselves from the standpoint of the loved one, as a worthy and esteemed person. Both of us, the giver and the receiver, the loving person and the loved one, have increased our respective gratifications. This process has the double function of increasing the amount of positive exchange in the social system at large as well as in each person involved.

LOVING: ITS PROCESS AND STRUCTURE

The process of loving as I have outlined includes a chain of contingencies in which the enactment of any one of them is somewhat dependent upon the realization of those preceding it. Thus, when any of the stated conditions are inoperative the process in general is impaired. The process requires each condition to be met in the order that it is presented. A summary of the process is presented in Figure 8–1. It can generally be described as (1) taking care of our own needs and security so that our own ego is not threatened; (2) accepting, empathizing, and being concerned about the needs of our loved ones; (3) satisfying their needs; and (4) empathetically feeling the gratification given to them.

In trying to become a loving person, we might go through this specific process. Perhaps we are frustrated sexually and our loved ones are frustrated economically. That is, we need sex and they need money. How would the process work?

First, we would have to realize that it is sexual deprivation which we have and not some other need which we have misinterpreted and have sexualized. We would then act in a manner which would gratify this need. If our loved ones could not help us, we would turn to one of our other sources.

Assuming now that each of our needs is satisfied, we would direct our attention to our loved ones. We would convince them that we would not reject them in any way for telling us their problem and their need and we would empathize with them about their situation. We would encourage them to develop alternative sources of income so as to provide them with more security in that need area. If we are their only source, we would then aid them according to our ability, supplying them with whatever financial support they need. The positive feeling we would get when they receive our economic help, as we empathize with their positive response, is the loving feeling. The satisfied feeling they experience is the satisfied feeling that we also experience as the process ends.

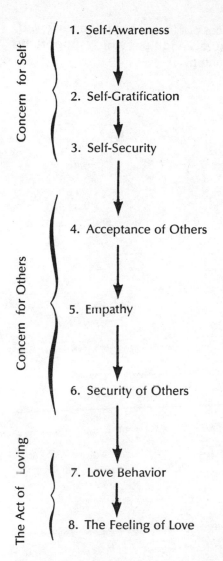

Concern for Self	1. Self-Awareness	The state of knowing our own needs, when they are frustrated, and how to satisfy them.
	2. Self-Gratification	The state of behaving in a manner that directly satisfies any frustrated self-needs.
	3. Self-Security	The state of having dependable alternative sources of need-gratification which can be elicited in time of deprivation.
Concern for Others	4. Acceptance of Others	The state of convincing our loved ones that they will not suffer in any way for revealing their secret thoughts, feelings, and acts.
	5. Empathy	The process of putting ourselves symbolically in the place of our loved ones and feeling, thinking, and responding as they would.
	6. Security of Others	The process of understanding our loved ones' need deficiencies and the desire to provide alternative sources for their gratification.
The Act of Loving	7. Love Behavior	The act of providing direct gratification for our loved ones' needs.
	8. The Feeling of Love	The state of feeling positive within ourselves as a result of symbolically satisfying ourselves and actually satisfying our loved ones.

FIGURE 8–1 The Process of Loving

In this chapter, the process of loving has been reviewed, but the value and social structural conditions which support the process still need to be evaluated.

9 THE SOCIAL FOUNDATIONS OF EMOTIONS

> Child-rearing practices, sexual attitudes, much religious dogma, attitudes toward material achievement, confusion about maleness and femaleness—all coalesce to make it difficult for an individual to learn to know himself, to like himself, to become acquainted with his real feelings and desires, and to learn to use himself more effectively and joyously.
>
> —William C. Schutz, *Joy*

Our emotions are aroused as we respond to our environment in a manner that deprives or satisfies our basic human needs. They are the inner subjective feelings produced by our actions which are in turn determined by our social surroundings.[1] If our environment provides rewards that satisfy our needs, we tend to behave by accepting these rewards and internalizing them as positive emotional effects. These effects constitute our state of feeling satisfied. Positive feelings include the emotions love, joy, contentment, elation, zest, compassion, serenity, and happiness which are results of our being gratified. The deprivation of our needs tends to result in negative emotions such as hate, fear, guilt, anger, shame, greed, hostility, anxiety, tension, jealousy, and frustration. Our emotions can then be classified as positive or negative depending upon whether or not our environmental conditions satisfy or fail to satisfy our needs. It might be interesting to classify kinds of environments into positive and negative categories, rather than our subjective emotional effects. A positive environment would consist of external conditions which bring about our need-satisfying behavior and feelings of love, joy, and so on. Negative environments would include those external conditions which bring about our need-depriving behavior and feelings of hate, fear, and so on.

Our emotions in general must be defined in terms of their behavioral and environmental preconditions, not only in terms of our inner subjective feelings. To attempt to understand our feelings independent of what causes them is not to understand our feelings at all, only to be aware of their existence.

We learn how we feel by watching others behave in certain social contexts. When we behave similarly under similar conditions we assume the way we feel is similar to the way others feel, that what causes a given feeling in us caused it in them. It is therefore other people's behavior and environment that give us the clue to their feelings and our feelings. In this manner we learn to identify and define our own feelings as they are affected by the kinds of conditions which had, in the past, affected others. These antecedent behaviors and social conditions thus add to our understanding.

Some of our basic emotions are defined below in behavioral and environmental terms. There is certainly room for more precision, but they do help us to understand the importance of specifying actions and social conditions leading to our inner feelings.

1. *Joy*. The feeling aroused after we behave in a manner that satisfies our needs in an environment which provides us with an adequate supply of rewards.
2. *Fear*. The feeling aroused after we behave in a manner avoiding social conditions which would deprive ourselves of need-satisfaction.

3. *Love*. The feeling aroused after we empathetically behave in a manner that gratifies another's needs.
4. *Guilt*. The feeling aroused after we behave in a manner that satisfied one of our needs, but the behavior is in opposition to what is socially expected.
5. *Resentment*. The feeling aroused after we behave in a manner that frustrated one of our needs, but the behavior is in accord with what is socially expected. Resentment complements guilt.
6. *Jealousy*. The feeling aroused after we behave in a manner that has produced our overdependency on one source of satisfaction and a state of competition exists for subsequent rewards from that source. Our jealousy is intensified as the commitment from our sole source is weakened.

My general assumption here is that feelings do not vary much from one person to another, given similar needs, behaviors, and social conditions. Feelings vary only to the extent to which, assuming our needs are constant throughout our species, our social conditions and behaviors vary. If we think certain feelings are desirable, they can be elicited by exposing ourselves to the corresponding social contingencies that cause the related behavior—and thus the feeling results. Our undesirable or negative emotions can be extinguished in a similar fashion. If we do not build the social structures that support need-depriving behaviors, negative feelings can be reduced. For example, if we desire to eliminate guilt, we must modify the social conditions so that all need-satisfying behavior is socially acceptable. Guilt then will never emerge. If we desire to eliminate jealousy, we must build the social structure so that overdependency on a single source of satisfaction is rejected in favor of multisource dependency. Along with this, our source commitment must be strengthened and cooperation must supersede a competitive situation where "winner takes all." I am suggesting that there are necessary conditions which lead to our feelings of jealousy. The probability of feeling jealous is increased when the following conditions exist:

1. Jealousy increases as the number of our sources of gratification in a given need area is reduced to one.
2. Jealousy increases as the strength of their commitment decreases.
3. Jealousy increases as the social norms and expectations promoting cooperative processes decrease.

These hypotheses are not exhaustive but they do provide some theoretical understanding as to the social causes of this emotion.

It is therefore possible for us to create a social environment where negative emotions are minimized and positive emotions are maximized. Our task is to discover and implement the social conditions and behavioral patterns that are most appropriate to this end. We should not have to suffer a great deal to appreciate the good feelings in life.[2]

There is already enough suffering in the world due to inadequate social conditions: enough disease, enough poverty, enough rejection, enough insecurity, enough conflict. Our primary concern could rather be hedonistic: to minimize pain and maximize pleasure. In the utilitarian tradition, it could be to provide "the greatest happiness for the greatest number." Our developing such a system would nevertheless produce periods of struggle and suffering. Change and growth are sometimes painful and, paradoxically, growing toward a system where there is less pain might be the only justification for pain to exist at all.

Our choice is either to suffer the pain of an inadequate social environment or to suffer the pains of change and growth. At least with change and growth there is a continuous reduction of pain. In fact, our growth might be defined partly in terms of gradually doing away with pain through expanding our awareness and appreciation, and cultivating new alternatives to satisfy our needs. It is sometimes painful for us to temporarily leave old sources of gratification in order to acquire the new, but when we can utilize and appreciate both the old and the new, we grow, and ultimately our pain is diminished. When our old alternatives are cherished to the extent that new ones are considered undesirable, or when our old alternatives are totally rejected in favor of new ones, we do not grow and pain becomes a normal part of life. Enduring our pain by failing to increase our number of alternatives for gratification is the absence of emotional growth and security, and is masochistic. As hedonists, on the other hand, we would be constantly looking for new ways to reduce our pain and increase our happiness and security.

In doing this we must examine the relationship between the amount of gratification we receive and the nature of the emotions that are being caused. We believe that the more gratification we receive, the more positive our emotional responses. The exception to this seems to occur when we have too much gratification. To eat too much is to become uncomfortable. To have too many friends is to become superficial and lose in-depth involvement. To have too much sex is to tire of sexuality. To have too much wealth is to become greedy and deprive others who may be in great need. In general, to have too much gratification is to become satiated, selfish, and not *truly* to maximize our own pleasure. Rather, our maximum pleasure comes with mild gratification, sometimes at variable intervals. For example, our joy and happiness are a function of our getting the amount of gratification we need when we need it, of not having to gorge ourselves for fear of being unable to satisfy our future needs. The greatest joy and happiness come with mild positive gratification when our needs demand. The kind of system that distributes rewards in this fashion produces secure, happy, and emotionally stable individuals. It is a system to strive for.

In other systems, some people get too much and others get too little. Neither are happy. Because the satiated, the rich, the sexually promiscuous, the heroes, all define themselves in terms of their affluence, their *raison d'être* is grounded in their squander. Their identity is tied up in their ability to *conspicuously consume.* They no longer see their affluence as a source of gratification in and of itself, but rather as a source of status. When others admire them for their greed and thus satisfy their need for self-esteem, they are motivated to further greed. When people are looked up to for being greedy (are rewarded for being overrewarded), those who are underrewarded are looked down upon. The rich are admired because they are rich and the poor are degraded because they are poor.

In a system where sanctioning extremes is common, our feelings also become extreme. Depression and elation, great joy and great sorrow, being "in love" and hating, conceit and self-contempt, extravagance and selfishness, sadism and masochism, guilt and resentment, passion and pain—these are all in part results of overgratification and undergratification. They are antagonistic, but in an extremist system, they go together.

> Actually our human passions are always connected with antagonistic passions, our [romantic] love with hate, and our pleasures with our pains. . . . It is because passion cannot exist without pain that passion makes our ruin seem desirable to us.
>
> Passion requires that the *self* shall become greater than all things, as solitary and powerful as God. . . . But hate of the other is likewise always present in the transport of the passionate love.
>
> But really a man becomes free only when he has attained self-mastery, whereas a man of passion seeks instead to be defeated, to lose all self-control, to be beside himself and in ecstasy.[3]

Our goal would not be to have great joy in one need area (satiation), but to have a little joy intermittently in each need area. Sorrow, as opposed to happiness, is losing dependable sources of gratification. We experience great sorrow when we lose our sole source of gratification; only mild sorrow when we lose one but have alternative sources available.

Thus our negative emotions are minimized and our positive emotions are maximized by decentralizing our need-dependencies and by reinforcing behavior in others that promotes the sharing of rewards so that no one is either satiated or deprived. Moderation in the number of sources of gratification we acquire as well as in the strength of rewards we receive serves as the key to maximizing our positive emotions. The feelings of love, joy, happiness, and compassion are moderated feelings, not extreme. They emerge when individuals are made to feel secure in themselves and are taught to be rationally and empathetically concerned for others.

If we experience strong feelings as a result of our own need-demands, behavior, and environmental conditions, we will not be in a position to feel as others feel. In order for us to empathetically feel, we must be in a rather neutral and stable emotional state. This, of course, presumes the conditions of ego-security and ego-loss discussed in the process of loving. Only when our own concerns are taken care of and a steady, mild, and positive emotional state exists are we ready for empathy. Both deprivation and satiation produce the strong emotions of pain and passion—and when we hurt we are preoccupied and in no position to feel for others.

Passion, an intense self-emotion, is not a state which contributes to our empathy or compassion. Compassion, on the other hand, can increase our own passion. Through the empathetic experience, emotions of others become our own. Our aim is to experience joy in the joy of others and sorrow in the sorrow of others, to make their passions our passions. Compassion becomes our own passion as we symbolically become others. Thus our own feelings plus our empathetic feelings maximize our total emotional experience. As we learn to feel our own joy as well as the joy of others, we become loving human beings, alive in the fullest sense of the word.

10 THE DIALECTIC OF INVOLVEMENT

The modern family has the threefold task of discovering individual and group values, organizing these into a meaningful hierarchy, and then integrating this new picture with the culture of which it is a part.

—Aaron Rutledge, *Pre-Marital Counseling*

Before asking what human values are, it seems important to ask what is of value to us as humans. What we value in common reflects our biological demands more than our cultural conditioning. Our bodily requirements, both material and psychological, are by far of more central concern than felt-needs defined by any given culture. These basic universal needs form the bases of the following discussion. It is self-evident that what we value most is their gratification.

Abraham Maslow argues that our needs arrange themselves in hierarchies of prepotency; the appearance of one need usually rests on the prior satisfaction of another more prepotent need.[1] Our survival needs are the most potent. Before we are at all concerned with our psychological well-being, we desire adequate food, clothing, shelter, drink, clean air to breathe, rest, body movement, and the like. Our lives depend on the rather immediate satisfaction of these needs, and since we usually want to live, these concerns tend to be of top priority. (Since we are so malleable however, we *can* be conditioned to want them frustrated and ultimately to want to die.)

When our survival needs are satisfied, we direct our attention to our safety needs. Here, we are interested in the maintenance of our survival through a more or less guaranteed future satisfaction. We wish to avoid pain and we seek an orderly environment in which responses toward us are predictable; an organized world which we can count on, one in which unexpected, unmanageable, or dangerous things do not happen to us. This typically includes our preference for a job with tenure, and our desire for a savings account and for insurance of various kinds (medical, dental, unemployment, disability, old age).

Our gratification of survival and safety needs is largely a function of the available wealth. The goods and services required to satisfy them are economic in nature and the modes of distributing them among people are expressed in economic and political ideologies. Our secondary needs, on the other hand, are psychological in nature and do not require a materialistic gratification. They first include our desire for community, love, affection, and a sense of belonging. In a search for psychic satisfaction, man

> . . . will hunger for affectionate relations with people in general, namely, for a place in his group, and he will strive with great intensity to achieve this goal. He will want to attain such a place more than anything else in the world and may even forget that once, when he was hungry, he sneered at love.[2]

Second, they include our desire for self-esteem. As we become part of the social setting, we develop a need for a stable, high evaluation of ourselves, for self-respect and the esteem of others. From the gratification of these needs, we feel self-confident, worthy, and capable; from their frustration, inferior, weak, and helpless.

Since our more psychologically based needs cannot be satisfied in a solely materialistic system, economic and political policies and practices are of little concern after they satisfy our more potent survival and safety demands. With basic needs met, our interests and efforts turn to the acquisition of a sense of belonging and self-esteem, and subsequently to self-actualization, self-realization, and self-autonomy. In the pursuit of rewards, we follow a logical sequence of concern, from our most primary needs to the full development of our personality.

If this pattern of need pursuit is characteristic of our species, it should be reflected in the development of our cultures. Then, economic and political matters would be the preoccupations of less technologically progressive societies. As these systems evolved to the point of providing adequate material satisfaction for the majority of the people, those who were gratified would become less concerned in the economy and the polity. The general interest in psychological gratification would then be a manifestation of social groupings most secure in their survival and safety. Nations with a highly developed technology and a strong middle class (in which the masses have acquired an adequate standard of living), would evolve a general desire for love and self-esteem.

What I am suggesting is that there exists a parallel between the hierarchical sequence of individuals pursuing their personal interests and the evolution of human culture. Our primary concern with material satisfaction is analogous to the almost total economic concern of primitive societies. Our psychic concerns are related to the growing interests of modern civilization with services and institutions designed to reduce psychological suffering. I will first deal with material gratification and its historical implications and then confront the evolution of psychological satisfaction.

MARXIAN DIALECTICS

Karl Marx has elaborated on a materialistic conception of history. Economic development, according to Marx, must pass through definite stages. Each stage has a distinctive mode of production and as opposing forces of production come in conflict with the existing mode, a new and more advanced stage emerges. This process of objective economic development is what Marx referred to as a *dialectic process.*

> The notion of a dialectic process Marx took over from the philosophy of Hegel and for Marx as for Hegel such a process has three stages. A "thesis" produces an entity opposed to it, the "anti-thesis"; the conflict between these two results in a "synthesis," which unites the opposing entities in a higher unity and itself becomes a "thesis" setting in motion a new stage of the dialectic process. . . .[3]

Marx then derived his basic laws of economic development from the dialectic process.

Marx's first major thesis (the existing mode of production in a particular stage of history) was to be found in the feudal system. The coercive caste structure in its repression and lack of social mobility provided the seeds of its own destruction as new (opposing) productive forces antithetically entered in the form of capitalism. The capitalist-feudal conflict gave way to a synthesized competitive class system and market economy (the new and more productive economy) where some vertical mobility was possible. The capitalist system then became the new thesis.

The capitalist economy, although it provided more gratification for the members of society in general, still allowed for the economic deprivation of the working classes. Marx envisioned the next antithesis to be the communist revolution. The communist system then evolved as a result of the excessive exploitation of the *proletarian* workers by the *bourgeois* merchants. The final synthesis, according to Marx, consisted of a communally controlled society where the principle of economic distribution would be "from each according to his ability, to each according to his needs."[4]

Marx's dialectic, in essence, traces the historical development of the distribution of materials which satisfy our needs. He sees the early stages as systems which centralize economic rewards in the hands of the privileged few and the final stage as a system which provides the greatest satisfaction of survival and safety needs for the greatest number. It is a review of the historical struggle of those people and classes of people who have had little wealth against those who have had more than they need, the conflict between the needy and the greedy — where the needy eventually win.

But "we do not live by bread alone." The Marxian dialectic deals only with the primary material elements. Once we secure our survival and safety, we seek emotional and psychological rewards. To account for the historical process of our subjective development, a new dialectic concerned with nonmaterial rewards is needed. It pertains to the distribution of esteem and acceptance rather than food and shelter. Furthermore, it is relevant to human striving only when our economic conditions have provided satisfaction for our survival and safety needs. It therefore follows the Marxian dialectical materialism in historical perspective.

In Figure 10–1, I attempt to represent the development of the dialectic process (both the old materialistic dialectic and the new psychological dialectic) during human evolution. The upper left part of the figure represents the earlier historical stages where the primary human conflict was over economic goods and services. In Maslow's need hierarchy, this period reflects deprivation in the primary need areas of survival and safety. It includes the battle between feudalism and capitalism, and then between capitalism and communism as suggested in Marx's dialectical materialism. The old dialectic dominating our history showed little concern for our higher psychological needs.

The center part of the figure represents current phenomena in the dialectic process. However, in some of the less industrialized and technologically advanced parts of the world,

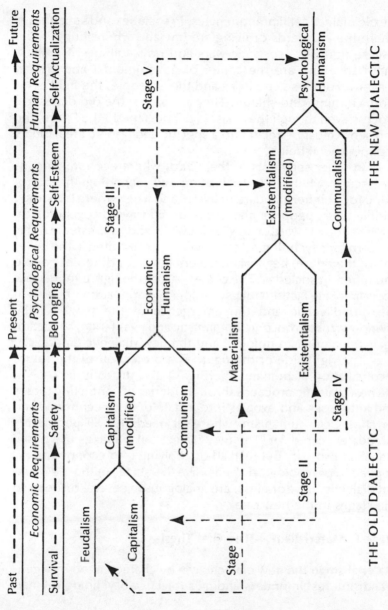

FIGURE 10–1 The Dialectic Process

the old dialectic still predominates. In societies and subcultures where the standards of living are low and where hunger and disease flourish, economic wars and riots still are of primary importance and are the center of governmental and civilian concern. For these countries and these people, the fight is for food, clothing, and shelter. They are part of the old dialectical process even though they exist in the present. In the figure, the "present" must be related to a specific geographic area and its economic well-being.

In other segments of the world, where economic needs are secure, where industrialization and technology have provided for a higher standard of living, and where there is a strong middle class, people's needs are turned toward psychological gratification, toward a desire for love and self-esteem. This concern for psychological satisfaction, represented in the lower half of the figure, begins at different times for different people and different societies. The center part of the figure represents economic satisfaction but psychological deprivation, the end of the old dialectic and the emergence of the new. As the economic forces become humanistic and egalitarian, a reaction against materialism unfolds, and the new dialectic emerges.

The right side of the figure is a projection of the future reconciliation of human suffering. Optimistic as it may seem, the new dialectic proceeds through a series of conflicting theses and antitheses and evolves into a state of both economic and psychological humanism, where all needs for all people are adequately cared for. The new dialectic also makes use of the Hegelian process, but instead of applying it to economics it is applied to psychological needs. The five stages in the old Marxian dialectic, nevertheless, are analogous in several respects to the stages in the new one.

Stage I: Materialism — The First Thesis

Materialism in the new dialectic can be characterized by a general disinterest in understanding subjective psychological matters as well as a disinterest in the feelings of identification and self-identity. It is both communistic and capitalistic. It is similar to feudalism (the corresponding first thesis in the Marxian dialectic) in that both systems allow vast deprivation in certain need areas — feudalism in the economic areas and materialism in the psychological. They both also are collectivity oriented; that is, they both emphasize the subservience of the individual to the larger social order. In this subservience, we are expected to accept our deprivation as a *given* and to concern ourselves with matters of interest to the state or the group. Strong controls are placed upon us to conform to existing practices and not to desire increased gratification in our respective need areas. Since there are no acceptable means for increasing our rewards, we are taught that being deprived of rewards is not necessarily bad. If we successfully adjust to our frustrations, we become masochistic, learning to fit into a social system which is not really concerned with our basic requirements.

Materialism tends to be more prominent among older people. It is especially strong among those of us who have lived most of our lives in an affluent environment, have successfully achieved some degree of affluence, or have been duped into believing that material gratification is the only kind of satisfaction worth striving for. As a result of being preoccupied with material things, we simple have not evolved an interest in the higher needs for love and self-esteem. Rather, we extend our surplus energies in the direction of physically isolating ourselves from social involvement by surrounding ourselves with more material objects. Our conspicuous consumption provides us with a larger estate, a bigger house with more and larger rooms, a larger and more beautiful television to watch. On top of this, we make rules and laws which restrict the number of other people to whom we can closely relate. Our almost fanatic desire for possessions, both property and people, sets the stage for our loneliness. Life seems to be meaningful when we have more than our share of material things, when these things can be isolated on our private estates, and when we can build a high enough fence around ourselves so as to prevent others from sharing. Needless to say this material greed and preoccupation with privacy do not bring us increased happiness. Unfortu-nately, many times it is the only way of life we know. But our psychological deprivation is extreme. We belong only to our property and our identity is threatened without it. We overcon-cern ourselves with material gratification and thus fail miserably to actualize our total human potentials. Our needs for psychological satisfaction are misdirected to things rather than people.

Stage II: Existentialism — The First Antithesis

Some of us in the more affluent societies eventually come to the realization that the accumulation of wealth and property is not bringing us the happiness that the communists and the capit-alists have promised. We develop an *existential* orientation. Existentialism is analogous to capitalism in several respects, even though most existentialists would deny it. Both capitalism and existentialism are opposed to the infringement of the social system upon the freedom of the individual. This antithesis is manifested in the *laissez-faire* notions of Adam Smith who ar-gued for free enterprise, void of government intervention. Indi-vidual freedom and responsibility advocated by many existen-tial writers reflect, in a similar sense, an abhorrence for au-thoritarian encroachment. Fritz Perls' dictum, "You do your thing — I'll do my thing," fits in here as a plea for less interven-tion on the part of others. Both capitalism and existentialism favor the rights and privileges of each of us over the collective interest, and believe that our free expression would lead to the greatest collective end. "The invisible hand," as Smith called it, ensures that our private interests and passions are led in the direction which is best for the whole society. Existentialist Jean-Paul Sartre likewise argued that "we always choose the good, and nothing can be good for us without being good for all."[5]

Another common concept of these two systems is that deprivation and struggle are natural, even necessary, steps to our fulfillment. We must suffer first and then through our individual effort and will, a higher state of need-satisfaction will come about. The Protestant ethic (if we work hard enough, material or spiritual rewards will result) is but an economic interpretation of the despair and the depression that the existentialist believes we must go through to reach a psychologically fulfilling state of "being." They both suggest that we are nothing else but what we make of ourselves. The primary difference between capitalism and existentialism is the content of the systems and not the form. Capitalism is concerned with economic gratification; existentialism is but a type of psychological capitalism.

These two systems then share many features: they are individualistic; they are suspicious of systemic intervention; they stress the volitional nature of people rather than the deterministic; they argue for uncontrolled freedom of expression; they imply that struggle is the means to fulfillment; they represent an active rebellion against social orders indifferent to our economic and psychological needs; they accept temporary individual suffering in the hope of later rewards; and they argue for social responsibility through self-interest, self-sacrifice, self-expression, and self-responsibility. Although neither system claims it, they are also similar in their heroism and self-glorification. Perhaps this is an overcompensation for an early state of deprivation. Because capitalists are at first without economic satisfaction, they must magnify their self-worth; because existentialists are without psychological satisfaction, they must magnify their self-esteem.

In their rebellion against established systems, both capitalists and existentialists tend to "protest too much." It is interesting to note that existentialists, in their hostility toward fascist and capitalist systems, fail to recognize the individualism, the struggling, and the heroism that they all have in common.

Both capitalists and existentialists have also learned to cherish for the sake of cherishing. Capitalists have learned that money and material things are valuable in and of themselves, independent of their function to satisfy others' needs. As capitalists love money for its own sake, existentialists love passion for its own sake. Passion is seen for what *it is,* not for what it does for others. The emphasis is strongly self-oriented; but since capitalists and existentialists are both deficiency motivated, what else can we expect? No wonder they cannot think of others' needs; they must each satisfy their own needs prior to incorporating a collective consciousness into their thinking. The ultimate danger, of course, is that existentialists will not stop when they are satisfied and move on to the next need area, but will instead overindulge themselves in their passions, just as capitalists have overconsumed material things. But when some get too much, others get too little. As conspicuous consumption on the part of some takes away from the gratification of others, so does excessive passion for its own sake take away from compassion.

The existential rebellion against materialism has nevertheless begun. The literary market is being flooded with books expounding the new, essentially nonviolent, revolution. These authors speak of a conscious rejection of the old culture and of its economic and technological emphasis. Philip Slater, a foremost sociologist, argues that

> the old culture . . . tends to give preference to property rights over personal rights, technological requirements over human needs, competition over cooperation, violence over sexuality, concentration over distribution, the producer over the consumer, means over ends, secrecy over openness, social forms over personal expression, striving over gratification, Oedipal love over communal love, and so on. The new counter culture tends to reverse all of these priorities.[6]

But our initial existential revolt against materialism is extreme. In our distrust for the prevailing social structure, we are almost anarchic. Our over-compensation for authoritarian repression is manifested in our dislike for *any* kind of socially imposed expectations, not just "sick" ones. As existentialists we want no controls or restrictions placed upon our behavior. We want to respond to our environment spontaneously, as we feel and as our will directs us. We want individual responsibility, not socially imposed responsibility. This provides us with justification for any kind of action, and we can refer to such action as being responsible since it is "true to ourselves." However, this individual responsibility functions no better in producing social responsibility on the part of existentialists than it does for capitalists when they are allowed to do what they want. The idealism sounds good, but it doesn't seem to work.

In our existential extreme, we also reject the acquisition of material wealth other than the "bare necessities." We become fanatically nonmaterialistic, arguing that the way to truth is found solely in our dedicated introspection, meditation, awareness of consciousness, or subjective inquiry. In ignoring objective reality, we typically turn to some form of mystical thought, and after enlightenment become true believers. (Religion is still the "opiate of the masses.") The alternatives to this are either our evolution to a less extreme position, or our complete schizophrenic escape from social reality. Some of us may regress, however, back to the conservative materialism of our parents' world.

The restrictive nature of our forms of monogamy and nuclear family has supplied some of the fuel for our primary existential revolution. As a reaction to puritanical monogamy we have turned to very superficial relationships (partial-temporary involvement). By not allowing ourselves to become too emotionally dependent upon any other person, we protect ourselves from getting hurt. A "sex for the sake of sex" attitude reflects our value of experiencing everything in life and living for the "here and now." We want no ties, just experience for the sake of experiencing. (Profit for the sake of profit!)

Stage III: Modified Existentialism—The First Synthesis

The synthesis of materialism and existentialism evolves as the materialists make concessions in the psychological need areas, and the existentialists come to recognize the value of the economy in maintaining their survival and safety. This synthesis incorporates the processes of appeasement, of compromise, of tokenism.

Out of our conflict between these two systems of thought, a new kind of market psychology is evolving. Our economic enterprises are becoming more and more interested in merchandising love and self-esteem; our productive forces are being redirected to providing us with better services rather than better goods. The do-it-yourself movement is one of the first indications of the industrial interest in self-esteem needs. Our increasing demand for psychological aid is also manifested in the popularity of various kinds of psychoanalysis, marriage counseling, and even "family therapy." Our emphasis is still on the satisfaction of psychological needs by treatment of the individual. Our assumption is still that the collectivity, the institutions, or the society is healthy and that the sickness is in the individual. We are still seen as being sick due to our personal inadequacies and lack of will.

In the modified existential view, however, collective aid for us is becoming institutionalized. The new psychological commodity is love, closeness, togetherness, self-awareness, self-worth, and self-autonomy. Sensitivity, encounter, and T-groupings are collective movements designed to provide us with such gratifications, in most cases for a fee. For larger fees, new corporate structures are emerging to meet the demand for love and self-esteem. Scientology, EST (Erhard Seminar Training), Mind Dynamics, Morehouse, Wailua, and dozens more to come will be the new religions. The commodity is always the same—self-identity and self-worth. The structure is based upon the exchange of self-insight and self-appreciation for a price—love of money. Surely this self-esteem for a profit can be referred to as psychological capitalism. At this stage the market is flooded with material commodities. If we desire to make a fortune, the marketable commodity is in convincing the customers that they are OK. People will pay a lot to gain this feeling.

Since it costs a lot, the market will at first be among the upper middle classes and then filter down to the middle and working classes.

The partial psychological satisfaction extended in modified existentialism is analogous to the partial economic satisfaction extended in modified capitalism. In the latter, collective efforts are made to appease our lower classes. The labor union movement, social security, and welfare programs of various types do not alter the basic structure of our capitalist economy but provide token satisfaction for our materially deprived, just as the existentially oriented encounter group movement supplies token satisfaction for our emotionally deprived. In neither case are we seen as both product and victim of the collectivity; rather, we are viewed as having individual inadequacies and thus unable to "pull ourselves up by our bootstraps." So the collective role, both in modified capitalism and modified existentialism, both in welfare programs and in encounter groups, involves helping people help themselves. Nowhere is there a hint of the ineffectiveness of the corporate structure itself, or of the structure of marriage and the nuclear family. In both modified forms, we are given temporary and partial gratification. We are not cured but are given a crutch—an illusion of satisfaction—a token. We have been co-opted by the system. This synthesis, nevertheless, is stabilizing in that the economically and the psychologically deprived are thrown a bone to keep them quiet. Appeasement works—at least for awhile.

The result of *modified capitalism* is the establishment of an economic class structure where some of us get more wealth than others. The rationale for these inequities is built upon the assumption that it is we as individuals rather than the collectivity who decide the amount of gratification we have, and we do this through our own efforts as a function of our volition. The result of *modified existentialism* is the establishment of a psychological class structure where some of us get more love and esteem than others. The rationale for these inequities is the same.

As the conflict between materialism and existentialism

becomes synthesized, a newer pattern of interpersonal involvement will accompany it. The extremes of centralizing our sexual-emotional dependency and our commitment on one person (monogamy) and its antithesis of superficially relating to many people will synthesize into a *total-temporary* involvement pattern. The total-temporary model does not eliminate the concept of possessiveness. In this model's serial monogamy, we become the property of one another for as long as we choose to remain together. This possession which is so characteristic of materialistic thinking, becomes marketable; that is, we can transfer it from ourselves to another in the process of contract and competition. The permanent availability of mates provides a setting where shifting involvement from one person to another is relatively easy. As a new suitor (competitor for sexual-emotional gratification) successfully alienates the affections of our mate, involvement is transferred from one to the other. We do not share mates, or commitments and dependencies. Competition for total involvement is still the mode. Love and esteem are the marketable commodities; total commitment is still the price. In modified capitalism, when we find a better product, the old is discarded. So too in modified existentialism, when we find a person who better satisfies our sexual-emotional demands, the old mate is discarded. Our commitment is withdrawn and extended to a newer and "better" product. Sometimes, however, mates are just loaned as in the case of wife-swapping—not unselfishly though, but for an exchange. Reciprocity is the norm in any market system, be it economic or psychological.

As materialism and existentialism are synthesized, a new social mechanism which allows for easy and ordered transfer of our involvement from one person to another emerges. Our growing acceptance of divorce, remarriage, and step-families is an indication of this trend. Along with this, the increased percentage of women working increases their exposure to alternative mates. Women, as a desirable and an emancipated "product," are much more appealing and available in the marketplace than in their isolated suburban homes.

Thus in the highly transient life style of the modified existentialists, a great deal of freedom is tolerated. We have the opportunity to search for new alternatives, new ideas, new acquaintances, and new identities. But as our materialistic concern is reduced, we reject our materialistically oriented families and are left with little social support. Since we have rejected most of the established forms of identification, we have lost most of our identity. So we look for a new meaning in life, but we have no place to go, no role to play, no position to hold, no expectations to meet, and no psychological rewards to gain. In our despair and loneliness, we travel around the countryside, living in near poverty, desperately seeking answers. We find little hope *around* ourselves, so many of us turn *into* ourselves. With a little help from our (transient) friends and perhaps "dope" of one form or another, we introspect, meditate, or invade our consciousness. We read literature and listen to music about people like ourselves and situations which are similar to our own. Because we have no particular future to look forward to, we live for the day that the answers will suddenly appear around the next bend in the road. Apathy, inaction, and even temporary reaction will accompany the despair and the futility during this stage.

It is this despair, this continued psychological frustration, that will eventually set the stage for the communal revolution. As in capitalism where the seeds of its destruction are found in the economically deprived segments of society, the seeds of the destruction of existentialism are found in the masses of the psychologically deprived. The establishment of an existential counter-culture with its do-your-own-thing orientation gives rise to a psychological class structure where those of us who can express ourselves adequately (usually through art, music, or poetry) constitute the upper class and receive an abundance of love and esteem at the expense of other less expressive people. "Everyone out of themselves" can then refer to a psychological rather than a material quest or, as it is reflected in the lyrics of a popular song, "everyone doing their own thing, don't care about you or me." The new existential culture, in its basically antiinstitutional framework (semianarchy) and its glorification of psychological individualism, will foster a society of the emotionally rich and the emotionally poor.

In our "escape from freedom" we (the new existentialists) speak of community. We attempt to organize communes which are void of competition and coercion. Most of our ventures have failed and I believe will continue to fail, due to the strong individualism ingrained in our thinking. If doing our own thing is contrary to the interest of the collectivity, our tendency is either to do it anyway or drop out of the commune.

> On this question the new culture talks out of both sides of its mouth, one moment putting the ideals of cooperation and community against old-culture competitiveness, the next moment espousing the old culture in its most extreme form with exhortations to "do your own thing." I am not arguing that individualism need be totally extirpated in order to make community possible, but new-culture enterprises often collapse because of a dogmatic unwillingness to subordinate the whim of the individual to the needs of the group. The problem is rarely faced honestly by new-culture adherents, who seem unaware of the conservatism involved in their attachment to individualistic principles.[7]

The outcome of these attempts to build community through individualism is a futility not fully understood nor adequately considered in existential literature. Suffice to say that it is as ridiculous for us to assume our general emotional satisfaction in a system founded upon unrestricted free expression as it is to assume our general economic satisfaction in a system based upon unrestricted free enterprise. When all of us are allowed to do anything we wish some of us will get hurt. It is of course those of us who get hurt the most who will provide the major support for the final revolutions whether they be communistic or communalistic.

As new existentialists, however, we will restore technology and science to their proper place as effective tools for social progress rather than as determinants and controllers of our existence. We will fully recognize that emotional well-being is not found only through economic well-being and will place both in a healthier perspective. We will maintain that a preoccupation with amassing possessions does not in fact reduce our loneliness. Perhaps our most significant contribution will be our movement toward self-awareness. For as we see ourselves more objectively, we paradoxically become aware of the absurdity of reaching happiness through only ourselves. This realization, that our self-contentment is found through the contentment of those around us, sets the stage for the communal revolution.

Stage IV: Communalism—The Last Antithesis

Communalism, like communism, can be characterized by our willingness to settle for less than everything we want in order to enjoy a number of things we really need. Here, we recognize that the collectivity has higher priority than each of us, but we see the group as being supreme only as long as it functions to promote the interests of us all, ideally in an egalitarian manner. As communists, we attempt to spread out material rewards somewhat equally among everyone, according to their needs, while as communalists, we attempt to establish institutions that provide for our general psychological gratification, again based largely upon need. Communists and communalists are also similar in that we both find self-assertion with no collective consciousness undesirable. Self-assertion for its own sake is discouraged. As a result we both encourage individual expression only as it contributes to the general welfare. Value is in utility as it satisfies our needs. Exploring better ways to share rewards is considered our highest form of activity. Doing other people's things is preferred to doing our own thing; understanding others' biases is encouraged more than dwelling on our own.

Another common characteristic of communists and communalists is a desire to build new social structures. We both are altruistic and utopian. In our revolutionary perspective, we reject the individualism described in Stage III and advocate a highly cooperative institutional framework. We both believe in making things public (including thoughts, actions, and property) rather than glorifying the concern for privacy so typical of the earlier stages. Our common concern for and our common ownership of property (including people as "possessions") is considered desirable.

One last similarity between communists and communalists is our de-emphasis on individual free will. Rather than adhering to the notions of self-determination, our behavior and attitudes are seen as a function of our social conditions. We are but a reflection of our individual environments. The means to change our personalities lie in the restructuring of the social contingencies in which we find ourselves. It is because of these values that as communists and communalists we are deeply concerned with building structures and initiating social processes which are congruent with the kinds of personalities we believe to be most healthy. In order to bring about a new social order, we feel that a temporary authoritarian kind of structure is needed. In this new structure, the more deprived segment of society would dictate to the individualists who have managed to gain more than their share of rewards. So the rule of the proletariat over the bourgeoisie in communism is analogous to the establishment of a dictatorship of the emotionally deprived. In setting up our communes, we as the emotionally deprived segments of society must build structures which will not permit psychological exploitation, just as communists have attempted to build structures which will not allow economic exploitation. Both of us, then, envision the gradual deterioration of centralized control and the eventual evolution of democracy and all its ramifications.

Since our marriage and family institutions provide many of the psychological rewards, we as communalists must concentrate on developing new structures that are designed to satisfy the needs and provide the functions usually assigned to these institutions. The family forms that we evolve, however, will be somewhat different. Institutions by definition are relatively *permanent* rather than *temporary,* so they imply long-term relationships. And because we as communalists are more interested in sharing involvement, our relationships will be *partial* rather than *total.* (The partial-permanent model is most appropriate at this stage.) We must develop some structure to insure enduring interpersonal involvement that is somewhat decentralized in dependency and commitment.

The change from monogamous marriage to experimentation in group marriage may well be the first indication that our new model for involvement is being activated. Such a shift in structure implies the breakdown of our nuclear family and its kinship ties in favor of a more extended form in which our family boundaries are not determined by blood lines. The purpose of these experiments, of course, would be to create an external source of identification for those of us who had previously and desperately turned inward. It is out of our loneliness and despair, our lack of social identity, our self-expressionism that ends in futility, that our communes will evolve. They will be many in number and in form. They will be large and small, rural and urban; they will be composed of the young and the old, the "straights" and the "hips"—but I believe most of them will probably fail after a short trial period.

I would attribute their failure to the strong existential influences that most of us have been reared under. Partly because we are more concerned with our freedom and dignity than with reducing our biases through a cooperative and systematically imposed environment, most of our attempts at this stage will fail.

> The usual kind of utopian-minded individual who seeks out such group marriages today is very frequently a highly peculiar, often emotionally disturbed, and exceptionally freedom-loving individual. But group marriage in many ways is not suited to this type of person, because it involves restrictions, restraints, and the kind of self-discipline that he has great trouble in achieving.[8]

The reconciliation of individual freedom and collective control is our primary theme in synthesizing existentialism and communalism. A series of paradoxes emerges in this process, which when actualized, leads into the last stage of development and into the core of a new morality and new family forms.

11 THE NEW NORMS: A FINAL SYNTHESIS

> A creature apart from a social group is nothing but an organic being. The member of a social group is a person, a personality developed under the molding influence of social interstimulation.
>
> —Ashley Montagu, *On Being Human*

Our final synthesis involves a merger of the old and new dialectics—an integration of economic and psychological concerns—into a general social humanistic system. Such a merger necessarily implies the reconciliation not only of the antagonisms between dialectical materialism and dialectical psychologism but also between a number of other antagonisms inherent in both dialectics. Included among these are the problems of freedom versus control, the individual versus the collectivity, unity versus variety, stability versus change, form versus function, and the ends versus the means. The reconciliation of each of these antagonisms suggests a logical contradiction. It would seem that to the extent to which one is practiced, the other must be extinguished. I don't believe that this is necessarily the case. The integration of these apparently opposite positions can be an essential part of a new normative structure, our new morality.

In our search for truth, we have historically found *absolute* truths. There would be nothing wrong with absolute truths if there were only one set of them. The problem is that we have as many absolute truths as we have different value systems—each maintaining that *its* absolute truth is *the* absolute truth. This leads us to the seemingly contradictory contention that perhaps our *only* absolute truth is that we have *no* absolute truths. If we assume that there are no absolute truths, then the most relevant question becomes how can we come closest to postulating an absolute truth?

FREEDOM IN CONTROL

The first reconciliation concerns the question of whether we are what we make of ourselves or whether we are the product of the culture that we have made. Do we have autonomy, free will, and self-determination, or are we a function of environmental contingencies and biological limitations? The arguments for and against these positions are extensively presented in philosophical literature. My concern is not in settling this dispute but more in the pragmatic question of the social implications of assuming one position or the other.

When we assume that our behavior is independent of our surroundings it destroys our motivation to design and build new social structures.[1] Assuming that we cause our own behavior motivates us toward introspection, meditation, egocentrism, and a general preoccupation with seeing the problems of our suffering in terms of our inadequacies. Self-blame and self-glorification detract from our movements to redesign institutions, communities, and societies. The assumption of self-determination is thus socially stagnating. It perpetuates the status quo. It is the philosophy of the materially and psychologically rich. The unfortunate aspect of this is that many of us who are economically and emotionally deprived have been duped into believing that self-determination is the answer to our deprivations. We become obsessed with the effects of the deprivation, namely ourselves, and completely ignore the cause—the social system.

Our belief in the deterministic premise (social causation), on the other hand, motivates us to modify the social system when it fails to provide for our general gratification. This is conducive to social change and growth and, subsequently, to our own change and growth.

The deterministic assumption, however, is nothing new. Many writers in diverse disciplines have defended it. The very cores of sociology and anthropology are based upon the notion of the sociocultural system being the cause of human misery or happiness. We will think, feel, and behave in one way under certain social conditions and not under others. But as individuals, can we do anything about effecting our own behavior and feelings?

The answer to this is yes, if we happen to have been exposed to an environment which has motivated us to (1) accept the deterministic assumption and (2) behave in a systematic manner which will bring about the appropriate rearrangement of our environmental contingencies. We don't do things because we *think* we should, or because we *feel* like doing them, but because we have been *socially conditioned* to do them. If, for example, we have been conditioned to smoke and also to want to stop smoking, our motivating environment might direct us to ask those around us not to reinforce us when we smoke. Assuming that those people who influence our behavior agree not to offer us a cigarette, light it, or give us any gratifying response as we smoke, our frequency of smoking might be decreased. Only in this manner might we be able to rationalize that we can modify our own behavior. The way to bring about a desired behavior is then to get ourselves in a social situation which rewards us for what we consider desirable.

But our responsibility as individuals is also in the direction of effecting others' behavior, feelings, and attitudes, not our own. What we reinforce in others through our rewards to them will effect their personalities. If we want to be effective in this area then we should understand the technology of building the social structural and interactional conditions which produce the kinds of individuals we desire. We can't do this by ourselves, however, since we are not the only influence on others. To completely determine their behavior, attitudes, and feelings we would have to control their total environmental exposure. Our personalities are then a product of a collectivity of people, both past and present, not a product of the simplistic explanation of individual will.

The causal pattern describing the human condition might be of greater interest to the scholar than the layman. It is summarized below; the steps proceed from the cause (1), with a constant (2), to the effects (3, 4, 5):

1. *Environmental contingencies* (independent objective stimuli) satisfy or frustrate
2. *Physical and psychological needs* (constant with the species), thus conditioning
3. *Behavioral patterns* (intervening objective responses) which in turn produce
4. *Emotional states* (dependent subjective conditions) and
5. *Attitudinal structuring* (dependent cognitive conditions).

It is our collective consciousness and our collective behavior that bring about the modification of environmental contingencies, and subsequently, the modification of individual deprivation, behavior, emotions, and attitudes. The collectivity causes; we as individuals are always an effect. Our contribution as a cause lies in our cooperation with others in redesigning and implementing new environments. We who are oblivious to our surroundings because of our preoccupation with ourselves can only be the product of others. We in this case are least free, for by ignoring the social conditions we allow others to design them for us. In their design we may be allowed less freedom. We become simply a victim of whatever kind of structure others create.

The individualistic philosophies, because they perpetuate the notion of self-determination, discourage us from participating in the creation of our own environment and thereby prevent us from effecting ourselves. *In promoting self-determination we have destroyed it. In believing in self-autonomy, we are losing it.* Philip Slater recently noted that it is a paradox of the modern condition that only those of us who oppose complete libidinal freedom can ever achieve it.[2]

The closest we can come to self-autonomy is first realizing that it cannot be achieved. We are truly free to the extent to which our individual environment secures our needs. In our belief that we are autonomous, and in our struggle to control our own destiny, we have reached a dead end.[3] The more we believe we are autonomous, the more blind we become to the kinds of social conditions that could lead us to greater freedom. Our freedom becomes more possible as we become aware of the necessity to change the structure of the environment which in turn effects a change in our behavior and personality. We are not free because we believe or feel we are free. We are free because we have been allowed by society to act free, and this allowance has given us a free feeling or a freedom of thought.

> Is man then "abolished"? Certainly not as a species or as an individual achiever. It is the autonomous inner man who is abolished, and that is a step forward. But does man not then become merely a victim or passive observer of what is happening to him? He is indeed controlled by his environment, but we must remember that it is an environment largely of his own making. The evolution of a culture is a gigantic exercise in self-control.[4]

Hopelessness, despair, and pessimism may be common for us as autonomous people for we persist in seeking identity within ourselves and thus avoid the objective origin and causes. In many instances we may have strong wishes for the destruction of any environmental forces acting upon us. If our environmen. tal influences were to be disordered, our behavior and thoughts too would become random as we internalize random stimuli. To argue that it is possible to have human happiness independent of our social environment is then the real absurdity.

> . . . he may choose the schizophrenic way and indicate that nothing he does is done in relationship to other people. The family of the schizophrenic establishes a system of rules like all families, but also has a prohibition on any acknowledgement that a family member is setting rules. Each refuses to concede that he is circumscribing the behavior of others, and each refuses to concede that any other family member is governing him. The attempt, of course, fails. The more a person tries to avoid being governed or governing others, the more helpless he becomes and so governs others by forcing them to take care of him.[5]

Control still exists even when we attempt to eliminate it. By refusing to become more aware of our influence on others, we do not diminish the influence, we just become more ignorant of interpersonal dynamics and less able to understand and apply knowledge in a more humane fashion. As we lose conscious awareness of the effect we have on those around us, our impact becomes not less, but less obvious. It is still there. Because we try to respond less systematically, we allow those who systematically apply behavioral technology to become the real directors of behavior. To ignore and be disinterested in our impact on others is thus to ignore our responsibility to them.

By rejecting the notion that we can influence, manipulate, or control others, we relinquish our ability to care for them. If we can't affect others, we can't do anything for them. By asserting the independency of others, we avoid our responsibility in socializing them. When we as parents attempt to rear children without the knowledge of behavioral technology, we are as incompetent and as irresponsible as the architect who is ignorant of civil engineering or the physician who ignores medical research. By not applying the principles of social technology in our everyday lives, a decision has been made for stagnation, apathy, and unconcern with modifying the present human condition. Thus our control of behavior, emotions, and attitudes is seen as something not only positive but necessary in producing more giving, loving, and cooperative children. Control in itself is not bad. "The problem is to free men, not from control, but from certain kinds of control."[6]

The control that produces frustration, deprivation, hatred, conflict, coercion, and the like is obviously not the kind of control we want. A system designed to eliminate these conditions requires a highly thought-out kind of control which, when implemented, takes on the appearance of less control. This occurs in a refined reinforcing system where our control is subtle, mild, and positive, but conscious; not in a system where control doesn't exist. The absence of control is chaos; it is ultimately coercive and therefore, I would suggest, quite undesirable.

I have argued that freedom is more appropriately an attribute of the social system. If we interact in a free system, we are free, or have freedom. If our collectivity is free, then and only then will we ever be free. The paradox is that our *freedom can be found only through control.* Our problem is to experiment, discover, and enact the kinds of social structures that will produce the freedom needed for greater human satisfaction. This is an endless endeavor.

SELF IN OTHERS

Our behavior and personality, being functions of our environment, require that we define ourselves in terms of those around us. The means by which we become more in touch with ourselves are through responding to ourselves and developing attitudes toward ourselves consistent with those expressed to us by significant others in our world. By internalizing their perception of us we can then value ourselves as they value us, like ourselves as they like us, and demean ourselves as they demean us. To see ourselves as they do reduces our alienation, gives us a more realistic self-concept, and aids in the development of a self that is social rather than schizophrenic. Only insofar as we take the attitudes of our organized social group toward the organized cooperative social activity or set of activities in which that group is engaged, do we develop a complete self.[7] A realistic conception of ourselves is thus impossible to the extent to which we avoid contact with others or negate feedback from them. Our insecurity and egotism produced by social rejection may lead us to believe that we can be determined by ourselves, but such an attempt is futile and self-destructive. In finding and developing our significant others, we find and create ourselves.

> Self-understanding is, paradoxically, self-transcendence, i.e. focusing one's interest and feeling upon the other in order to discover what his words, gestures, and posture mean to him. . . . Self-understanding conceived as social feeling means to see one's self (insight) by participating with another, sharing mutual concern, or more succinctly, being an "I" for a "thou" as Buber would say. It is precisely in such an "I-thou" relation that one is able to establish the necessary distance between himself as figure and his self-seeking pragmatic involvement as ground, for self-understanding to come about. Schutz, the late social philosopher of common sense life, comes to a similar conclusion through a phenomenology of face-to-face relations: "I experience myself through you, and you experience yourself through me."[8]

Our dependency and interdependency are thus indispensable conditions of life—and these are the conditions which all living organisms strive to maintain.[9] If we are at all independent, it is only because and perhaps to the extent that we have dependencies upon others. It is the pattern of relationships that we have established with others that allows us a sense of independence.

As these interrelationships dissolve, we become more dependent, not less. We are thus not independent because we decide to be independent but rather because we are securely integrated into an interdependable social system. Our realization of the necessity for maintaining these dependencies does not result in despair. On the contrary, when such realizations do occur, they provide us with the direction we need to build a secure pattern of interpersonal relationships.

There is thus a close relationship between how we feel, think, and act toward others and how we feel, think, and act toward ourselves. We accept and are aware of ourselves to the extent to which we accept and are aware of others. We hate in ourselves only what we hate in others. If we are unable to care for anyone or anything separate from us, we are unable to care for ourselves.[10] Our respect and love for ourselves are thus a direct function of our respect and love for others.

In review, I will suggest the second paradox: the *self can be found only through others.* For us to seek selfhood or individuality is one thing. To seek community is another. But to attain "individuality in community," where we grow because we help others grow, where our interest is in the interest of others, is one of the primary aspects of the new norms.

UNITY IN VARIETY

In our understanding the whole of anything, generalizations must be induced from its parts. Our creative acts are the rearrangement of old parts into new patterns. Any creation or invention is defined in terms of its newly developed interrelationships. When we attempt to isolate any given part of a system and define it only in terms of itself, understanding is reduced. In another sense, things do not cause themselves, they are caused by other things. The interrelationships among a variety of things surrounding an object, living or nonliving, can best define and explain its nature.

The philosophy of science is founded partly upon this assumption. Scientific knowledge is discovered by observing a variety of factors in a variety of states and subsequently deriving probabilistic statements about their totality. It is the variability in natural phenomena which allows scientists to predict events and understand what causes things to occur. It is the variability in the states of things around us which allows us to know them. Statistical models are sometimes defined in terms of whether we are right when we say we are (accuracy estimate) divided by the extent to which we are wrong when we say we are right (precision estimate or estimate of error). They are an estimate of *unity* divided by an estimate of *variability*. Science is the search to discover unity in the variety of nature—or more exactly, in the variety of our experiences. B. F. Skinner, probably the best known behavioral psychologist, has taken a similar position in arguing that it is science or nothing, and the only path to simplification is to learn how to deal with complexities.[11]

I already noted that an accurate concept of self can be found only through feedback obtained from a variety of others. Perhaps a random sample of others knowing us and relating to us would provide an unbiased and most objective picture of what we really are. Social isolation, of course, allows us only to contrive a hopelessly biased picture of ourselves. Becoming involved with a variety of people, we can not only increase our security by diffusing our dependencies but receive more unbiased and generalized feedback.

In varying our social contacts, we also provide a situation where our need for love is best satisfied.

> Those who have been adequately loved feel free to look out upon and embrace the world with interest and compassion. They brook no hostilities to human diversity, and are opposed to any form of downgrading standardization. They see likeness and unity in difference, and do not equate unity with uniformity. They regard differences as points of interest, as complementary and not as antagonistic, as the means, indeed, of a more abundant common life, of sharing and cooperation.[12]

On the other hand, it is the unloved individual who most fears the extension of his involvements to new kinds of people and diverse groups. As an unloved person we are a product of social rejection and isolation. The more we seek privacy and define ourselves in terms of ourselves, the more alienated and lonely we get. Our unity, our wholeness, our totality—these do not exist, for the diverse influences which make up a healthy individual have been separated from us. We are not a product of diversification but of narrow exposure and self-appraisal. We do not have unity—only uniformity. We see our self-appraisal as a reflection of individualism but, as Slater has noted, individualism itself produces uniformity.[13]

This paradox is that *unity can be found only through variety.* As designers of new social forms we must be concerned about the continual provision of diversification in structuring our institutions. Many of the prevailing codes in society allow little room for this. Among other things, we as innovaters must seek

> . . . wholeness, and obviously [we] cannot achieve this by exclusion. A [family] that does not have old people and children, white-collar and blue-collar, eccentric and conventional, and so on, is not a [family] at all, but the same kind of truncated and deformed monstrosity that most people inhabit today.[14]

STABILITY IN CHANGE

The notion that our most stable institutions are the most static and rigid is outmoded. Stability is not found in the status quo nor, on the other hand, is it found in revolutionary change. Although revolutions are sometimes necessary to break up stagnating social forms, radical structures do not seem to work well immediately following the upheaval. Some of the tactics and practices used in the old regime are commonly implemented by the new power but the real ideals of the revolution come into existence over a longer period of time. It is in the evolutionary stages following the revolt where the stability of the system is established. When the evolution stops, stagnation and rigidity tend to set in again—and perhaps, in time, another revolutionary movement will emerge.

We can prevent stagnation or revolution by establishing a constantly evolving system where experimentation, innovation, and curiosity are a part of everyday living. When the social system stagnates, we stagnate; when it is upset, we are upset. When the system changes and grows, we do the same. The paradoxical condition is that the most stable social system we can build is one where mechanisms designed to modify it are built into it, one in which *stability can be found only through continuous change.*

Our new norms must incorporate the idea that the only thing which is constant is that everything changes and that instability occurs when flexibility is not allowed. Stability within ourselves can be maintained only through our change and growth, and that requires that our environment be designed for such a purpose. Our new values must support an evolving, mobile, rotating institution where we are able to move in and out, are born and die, terminate relationships and create new ones. It must be a permanently changing structure, stationary in its flexibility and constant in its dynamics. Our conception must be highlighted as an environment where human gratification is our goal and creativity and experimentation our means.

FORM IN FUNCTION

In the process of creating, we must consider the structure or form which the creation will take on. Artists of all persuasions for many centuries have asked the questions, "What is good form?" and "What is beauty?" Beauty or good form to the individualist, for example, is "in the eye of the beholder." It is whatever we as individuals believe it to be. A tree is beautiful because we like it. Beauty then is individually validated, for our taste is the criterion. It is, more realistically, nothing but a function of our own prejudices or biases—or more euphemistically, our own preferences and tastes. Using such a definition of good form thus encourages us to develop more biases, for to rid ourselves of biases is to rid ourselves of what beauty is all about!

Another concept of beauty pertains to the existential notion that things are beautiful *in and of themselves.* Things are beautiful because they exist. A tree is beautiful just because it is a tree. It would seem to follow logically that anything that exists is therefore beautiful or has good form. Not only is such a position conservative (since all existence is beautiful, we should conserve all of it) but it is partly sadomasochistic in that the deprivation, pain, and suffering existing within each of us must also be thought as beautiful, not to mention the many objective causes of our misery. This position, in a way, justifies anything for its own sake. "Form for form's sake" can then be expanded to "art for art's sake," "music for music's sake," or "passion for passion's sake." This might be fine—but what about "pain for the sake of pain" or "war for the sake of war"? When any form is good, all forms can be justified as good.

A third way of looking at good form is in terms of its function. Something is beautiful, not for what *it is,* but for what *it does.* It is beautiful to the extent to which it functions. It would be more appropriate here to say that something *works* beautifully than to say that something *is* beautiful. Although the function of a tree, in itself, is to grow and be nourished, from our perspective, the tree would not be beautiful because it existed or because it looked nice, but rather because it provided shade from the heat of the sun, or fruit to eat, or lumber to build a shelter.

If our function is to live, to be nourished, and to avoid suffering, then we are beautiful to the extent that we fulfill this function. That which causes us pain, as well as pain itself, is ugly. That which causes us pleasure (without causing others pain) is beautiful. Human pleasure (need-gratification) is then all that is beautiful in and of itself, since pleasure adds to the human function—and pain detracts from it.

To the extent to which we become sidetracked from the direct gratification of universal human needs and spend our time and energies on nonfunctional activities, we reduce ourselves to ugliness. We are, in fact, caught up in producing ugliness in many ways under the pretense that what we have created is good *in and of itself.* Instead of learning to evaluate others' beauty in terms of their actions and thoughts (functioning), we have become preoccupied with modifying their form so that they look nice or behave to fit our biases. We expend tremendous resources decorating our bodies, automobiles, and homes with objects that are useless in gratifying our basic needs. We are surrounded with jewelry, frilly clothes, cosmetics, rococo cornices and columns, chrome-plated and glass-blown dust collectors, as well as devices such as paintings, novels, stereos, and TV sets with which we can escape our frustrations. These are the things that make us pretty people in pretty surroundings.[15] These are the things which are valued when we define beauty in terms of *what is* or *what we like.* When we are beautiful just because we *exist,* we tend to decorate ourselves as we are and reinforce our prejudices as they are. On the other hand, when we are beautiful for what *we do,* we can observe our behavior and our thinking and ask if they contribute to the gratification of our needs. It is this gratification that makes us feel good, that makes us beautiful. From a functional perspective, our importance is defined in terms of *how well we exert effort* in producing need-gratifying conditions for ourselves and others, not in terms of *who we are,* how good we look, or what position we happen to hold in the social hierarchy.

There are three ways in which we as artists can function to gratify our needs; they are analogous to the three involvement patterns discussed in Chapter 5—self-, reciprocal-, and love-involvements. The first, *self-expression,* occurs when we create form for the sake of creating form. This is commonly rationalized as "I create whatever pleases me; I don't care if you like it or not." More than likely we are getting or have gotten some attention for our efforts but we nevertheless maintain that our motivation originates from our inner self. Our purpose is not to communicate, but rather to express ourselves. If we are painters, our paintings may be totally abstract; if musicians, our music may be so loud that the lyrics cannot be heard; if poets, our writing style may deviate quite a bit from standard grammatical form and dictionary definitions. We refer to this as creative artistic expression, but in effect our message can be interpreted in as many ways as there are people who observe it, for people read their own meanings into our message. Our form then becomes nonoffensive to our patrons. They in fact enjoy it as a mechanism by which they receive reinforcement for their own tastes or prejudices. As a result of this, we receive monetary or attentive rewards. But we fail to communicate our specific message (assuming that we had one) and, of course, avoid direct effective communication with our patrons.

As the second kind of artist we are somewhat more honest in creating our forms. In our *commercial-expression,* we are at least willing to admit that the primary intent of our art is not so much to express ourselves as to please others (reinforce their biases), so that they will in turn reward us with fame or fortune. We are not concerned with whether or not our patrons *need* our creations, only that they *want* them. We trade what they think they need for what we think we need. Unfortunately, because most of us are unaware of what we really need for a happy life, we usually end up producing products that further decorate ourselves or our homes, or provide means and gadgets by which we can escape our frustrating reality.

As the third kind of artist we are concerned with *love-expression.* We receive gratification in creating a form which can be used to directly satisfy the real needs of others. By "direct satisfaction" I am referring to processes which provide more nutritious food; clothing designed for warmth and comfort; architecture designed and built for safety, efficiency, and economy; better medical research and technology; increased sexual pleasures; more knowledge about interpersonal relations and behavioral engineering; and perhaps most important, designs for new institutions which will more effectively facilitate these processes. Along with this, any form which supports the gratification of these basic needs is also within the limits of our love-expression. As a love-oriented artist we are always conscious of the function of our creations as they satisfy human needs. To us, *form can be found only in function,* and our function is our gratification. Our aesthetic sense has a lasting value only when it promotes the well-being of humanity.

Our new norms maintain that it is vital for everyone to try to become more loving in our artistic expression. Our reward for this, of course, is a greater sense of belonging to each other and to the human race. In loving others by creating and caring for their needs, we in turn come to love and esteem ourselves. When our own needs are secure and we are ready for growth we will not want to expend our energies in expressing ourselves by entertaining others or escape by being entertained by others. We will rather become active participants in living rather than passive frustrated entertainees. As growth-oriented people we will not be primarily concerned with expressing our own preferences and tastes and will not be interested in sacrificing communication for "good style." We will be interested in creatively developing messages which transfer meaning among us more effectively (are not subject to many interpretations) and in innovating in a cooperative and antibiased manner. We will socialize children to express themselves creatively so that the direct need-gratification of each of them occurs through the direct need-gratification of others. Our beauty is in each of us helping ourselves by helping others.

ENDS IN MEANS

In some of our traditional philosophies, "the ends have justified the means." Believing we had found the absolute truth, any method to perpetuate and extend it was conceived as being justifiable. When we do not have the absolute truth, however, the ends themselves are unknown, or at least are in doubt. If our ends, goals, or objectives are in question and perhaps unattainable, we have little choice but to emphasize the means by which our truths can be approached, rather than glorifying the truths themselves. In this case our means justify our ends rather than our ends justifying our means. The methods, the processes, the functioning, the thinking, and the behaving are the *means* by which conclusions, structures, and forms become *ends*. *How* something is done defines *what* it is. How we think determines what we think, how we function defines what our structure is, and how we act reflects what we are.

Because our new values deny absolute truth (an end in itself), objectives are founded upon human functioning, upon methods of thought and social interaction—*the ends can be found only through the means*. By applying methods of thought to the problems of our functioning (deprivation and satisfaction), structures, norms, and patterns of behavior can be created to form a new social order; the means lead us to the ends. I have already discussed the human function. How we think and how we act to create new structures are our immediate concerns.

Although our new norms reflect some conclusions and some social structures, these conclusions and structures are in no manner to be considered total, perfected, or eternal. The essence of our new value system pictures truth as conditional, tentative, probabilistic, relative, and subject to error and doubt. Our methods of thought incorporate a self-correcting mechanism producing a constantly evolving body of knowledge.

Although our thought patterns in a general sense are rational and have been derived from logic and the philosophy of science, they can also be expressed in paradoxical form. For example, the only thing we know for sure is that we don't know anything for sure. The only *right* way of thinking is that we could be *wrong*. The only thing we should not doubt and criticize is that we should doubt and criticize. The only thing we should be prejudiced against is prejudice, and we should tolerate tolerance and be intolerant of intolerance. The ends thus are *in* the means. What to think is in how to think. The value is in the process. "The joy is in the journey."

Therefore, conclusions, truths, forms, and structures, as ends, are never sacred. If anything is sacred, it is the means by which our ends are obtained—and there is some doubt about that! A note of caution might be offered at this point. We should be aware of the negative consequences of carrying anything too far, of going to extremes. Thus, although our freedom can be found only through control, too much control can be coercive. Although the self can be found only through others, focusing too much on others can block our self-awareness. Although unity can be found only through variety, too much variety can lead us to superficiality. Although stability can be found only through change, too much change is disorganizing. Although form can be found only through functioning, too much emphasis on functioning can lead us to lose track of what the relevant function is. Although the ends can be found only through the means, too much concern with the means can leave us with no conclusions. Too much or too little concern with control, others, variety, change, functioning, or means can limit our freedom, individuality, unity, stability, beauty, and goals. Extremism exists only in the earlier stages of human evolution. Moderation and evolution are the key words in our new normative system.

These reconciliations constitute our final synthesis of the old and new dialectic forms. They fuse the traditional conflicting values into an integrated whole and provide the foundation for our new normative system. These new norms are not easy to comprehend nor can they be easily projected as a part of some futuristic social system. They do, however, provide us with some clues as to what the nature of interpersonal relations and family living might be. They suggest that the structure of families

will become more flexible, more democratic, more cooperative, more rational, and more functional. They indicate that the
transition will involve going beyond the notion of self-
autonomy, beyond human deprivation, beyond absolute
truths, beyond jealousy and possessiveness, and along with
these trends, beyond monogamous marriage and the nuclear
family structure.

Epilogue

And to others of good will, who want to help make
a better world, I recommend strongly that they
consider science as a way of doing this, a very good
and necessary way, perhaps even the best way
of all.

—Abraham Maslow, *Motivation and Personality*

There are many advantages of our communal family structure,
and perhaps as our needs and social conditions change there
will be an increasing number of disadvantages. Our important
realization is that there is a general causal relationship between
social conditions and their effects as our actions, emotions, and
thoughts are shaped. As new behaviors and new methods of
gratifying needs evolve, as science and technology become
more advanced, and as industrialization, urbanization, and
communication progress, the structure of our communal family
or of any family must be redesigned and refined—if we are to
continuously bring maximum happiness to ourselves.

Understanding how our social structure determines our
personalities is all-important in designing and building a better
world. If our structure is ineffective, it will be reflected in us. If
there is poverty either economically or psychologically, the
social forms under which we live will need some revision. To
consider any structure as sacred and unalterable is to ignore our
changing needs, especially in our rapidly changing world. If we

fail in building effective social structures, we fail in building our gratification, security, and love.

The humanistic psychologists including Abraham Maslow, Carl Rogers, Erich Fromm, and Jean Piaget have devoted much of their work to describing the more ideal personality. They tell us rather elaborately about the product of a healthy social system—the self-actualizer, the self-realizer, or the autonomous person—but they say very little about the social conditions that produce these kinds of people. I get the feeling that these superqualities just seem to exist in some of us and not in others, or that we somehow just decide to make them part of ourselves—perhaps by exerting our initiative, motivating ourselves to great heights, or simply deciding we are going to become that way—as if our environment had little to do with it. Related to this view, we are immediately reminded of the capitalistic myth that affluence is but the natural end of self-determined ambition (shades of the Protestant ethic and Horatio Alger). Our idea of free will perpetuates this myth. Our sacred institutions are freed from blame and allowed to impose their injustices upon the masses of co-opted individuals.

Our answer is not in describing what a healthy person is, for we all know what healthy people are—they are people who are happy because they have their needs satisfied and feel secure that they will continue to have them satisfied. Our problem is designing and building institutions that will produce these happy people. What we need are healthy social structures that will maximize our gratification, and then as self-actualizing and autonomous individuals we will emerge en masse.

As autonomous people we have to realize that no one is autonomous. We have to be aware that we are a product of our genetic heritage and our individual environment. We must attempt to discover and understand the social conditions which cause us to feel, believe, and behave the way we do—or would like to. With these realizations comes our motivation to create the kind of environment where others will reinforce our positive feelings, cooperative values, and loving behavior. As we are exposed to this environment, we become more and more aware that independency implies superficiality and uninvolvement, and that overdependency breeds insecurity, jealousy, and possessiveness. We see that interdependency or a somewhat diffused dependency provides us with the maximum amount of freedom, mobility, love, growth, and security.

We must feature ourselves unique only to the extent to which our heredity and environment are unique. We must realize that our motivation to grow and change has been implanted in us by our social history. We must accept the assumption that we have been shaped into what we are rather than cling to the conventional free-will explanation (or lack of explanation) of why we do what we do. We must further realize that it is those of us who are misled, insecure, threatened, and deprived who tend to glorify ourselves and explain ourselves in terms of ourselves rather than see ourselves as interdependently connected to external conditions. It is no wonder *self-determinists,* especially those of us who have not received our share of the economic or psychological rewards, develop feelings of helplessness, futility, and pessimism, since we must blame ourselves for our own failure, our own frustrations, our own destiny. To me, this line of thinking is depressive, masochistic, and perhaps suicidal.

The only apparent way out of this existential dilemma is to stop blaming ourselves and stop searching inwardly. Rather we must strive for an understanding of our *social* selves and see our frustrations as a function of our frustrating environment, of the institutions which overgratify some of us and undergratify the rest. Paradoxically, we who are first to zealously argue our autonomy are probably least autonomous because of our blind denial of the socially and biologically rooted factors which have caused us to be what we are.

SCIENCE AND HUMANISM

There has been a recent trend in countercultural literature to equate science and technology with materialism and the established society in America. Theodore Roszak, for example, characterizes science as involving a "myth of objective consciousness." He argues that

> . . . some of the leading mentors of our youthful counter culture have, in a variety of ways, called into question the validity of the conventional scientific world view, and in so doing have set about undermining the foundations of the technocracy.[1]

To assume that science as a philosophical system and as a way of knowing can be identified with the established society is nothing short of a complete misinterpretation of what science is all about. Science is, and has been from its inception, a radical philosophy. Tentativeness, skepticism, relativity, intersubjective validity, tolerance of new alternatives, and probabilistic determinism—characteristics of science—have never constituted the basic value system or the prevailing order of any society in our history. The old culture and institutions in the Western world can better be described in terms of a scientific antithesis than in terms of science itself. They tend to perpetuate such values as absolutism, acquiesence, the assumption of eternal truths, subjective validity, the sacredness of existing structures, rationalization for prejudices, some form of spiritualistic bases for gaining knowledge, and our inherent free will. In most of these respects the youth involved in the counterculture are much more conventional in their values than science has ever been. They change from one religion to another, from one set of prejudices to another, from one kind of conformity to another, but they still hold to the notions of free will and the spiritual and subjective sources of truth. To separate science from the countercultural movement is not to make science more conventional, but rather, to make the counterculture less radical than it appears.

Technology or engineering (the application of scientific knowledge) has also been identified with the established order. It is certainly the case that the political, industrial, and military institutions have used technology to bring about changes. But the type and direction of change must be differentiated from the effectiveness of technology as a tool. We must be careful not to abandon the tool because we do not like the product. Does it make sense to discard a hammer because we don't like the house someone built with it?—especially if we don't have a better way to pound nails! Technology itself is neutral. It can be used to make us feel good or it can be used to destroy us. How it is used is determined *not* by the technology itself but by the political and economic ideology of the institutions and societies that apply it.

For the countercultural movement to condemn science and technology and to link them necessarily with the establishment is to confuse the means with the ends, the tool with the product, the valuable knowledge and the techniques for applying that knowledge with how they are being applied and to what ends. Science and technology have been used to destroy millions of people during wartime, but they have also been used in medicine to save millions more. To what end we use these tools is our primary question. Their value and effectiveness as tools are well documented. Who, for example, would want to eliminate medical technology? I am sure that a countercultural youth would need hospital services in the case of appendicitis. The obvious point is that science and technology are means to any number of ends. Discarding a valuable tool along with an undesirable product is a rather foolish gesture.

It seems that our real problem lies in our older generation's preoccupation with material gratification and overgratification. Science and technology can be used to produce affluence but the values of conspicuous consumption, greed, and the worship of objects are certainly not their essential constituents. This preoccupation with material needs and their overcentralization in the hands of a select portion of society, along with the failure to understand and effectively gratify psychological and social needs, are more the real complaints of the counterculture. Our rebellion should be directed at the causes of the problems. Our target should be the prevailing ideology which values material objects far beyond their basic need-gratifying functions, not the scientific method; it should be how the material wealth is distributed in society and the criteria used for distribution, not the technology used to produce it.

Science and technology can be used to increase gratification in our social and psychological need areas, just as in the economic areas. We must alter our ideology and develop new structures that will gratify everyone rather than overgratify some and deprive others. Our answer lies in a more humanistic ideology where our needs, both material and psychological, and their satisfaction through cooperation and love, are the primary ends; and where science and technology, as the most effective tools available, are the primary means to achieve these ends. "A Scientific Humanism emerges as a philosophy holding considerable promise for mankind—*if* mankind will at all succeed in growing up."[2]

Notes

Chapter 1

1. Mervyn Cadwallader, "In Search of Adulthood," in *Teenage Marriage and Divorce,* eds. Seymour Farber and Roger Wilson (Berkeley: Diablo Press, 1967), p. 19.

2. U.S. Bureau of Census, *Statistical Abstract of the United States, 1964* (Washington, D.C.: Government Printing Office, 1964), p. 31; U.S. Department of Health, Education, and Welfare, Health Resources Administration, Rockville, Md., *United States Vital Statistics Report* 22, no. 5 (25 July 1973).

3. Simone de Beauvoir, *The Second Sex* (New York: Bantam, 1953), p. 452.

4. Albert Ellis, "Romantic Love," in *Reflections on Marriage,* ed. William Stephens (New York: Thomas Y. Crowell, 1968), p. 75.

5. Snell Putney and Gail Putney, *The Adjusted American* (New York: Harper & Row, 1964), p. 127.

6. Putney and Putney, *Adjusted American,* pp. 117–118; Eleanore Luckey, "Number of Years Married as Related to Personality Perception and Marital Satisfaction," *Journal of Marriage and the Family,* 28, no. 1 (February 1966): 44–48.

7. De Beauvoir, *Second Sex,* p. 418.

8. George Levinger, "Marital Cohesiveness and Dissolution: An Integrative Review," in *Families in Crisis,* eds. Paul Glasser and Lois Glasser (New York: Harper & Row, 1970), p. 120 and p. 124.

9. Charles Ackerman, "Affiliations: Structural Determinants of Differential Divorce Rates," *American Journal of Sociology* 69 (July 1973): 13–20; T. W. Adorno et al., *The Authoritarian Personality* (New York: John Wiley, 1950), p. 614 and p. 757; Bert Adams, *The American Family* (Chicago: Markham, 1971), p. 295.

10. De Beauvoir, *Second Sex,* pp. 450 – 451.

11. Jesus Rico-Velosco and Lizbeth Mynko, "Suicide and Marital Status: A Charming Relationship," *Journal of Marriage and the Family,* 35, no. 2 (May 1973).

12. James W. Prescott and Cathy McKay, "Child Abuse and Child Care: Some Cross-cultural and Anthropological Perspectives." Unpublished paper presented at the National Conference on Child Abuse, 7–9 June 1973.

13. Ellis, "Romantic Love," p. 76.

14. William Goode, "The Theoretical Importance of Love," *American Sociological Review* 24, no. 1 (February 1959): 46. Although the control of kin is more removed in the nuclear family than in the traditional extended structure, a more democratic model necessitates a complete removal of kin control from the family unit.

15. Nicholas Babchuk and Alan Booth, "Voluntary Association Membership: A Longitudinal Analysis," *American Sociological Review* 34, no. 1 (February 1969): 31.

Chapter 2

1. Hans Sebald, *Adolescence: A Sociological Analysis* (New York: Appleton-Century-Crofts, 1968), p. 51.

2. U.S. Bureau of the Census, *Statistical Abstract of the United States, 1972* (Washington, D.C.: Government Printing Office, 1972), p. 39.

3. E. E. LeMasters, *Parents in Modern America* (Homewood, Ill.: Dorsey Press, 1970), p. 4.

4. F. Ivan Nye, John Carlson, and Gerald Garrett, "Family Size, Interaction, Affect and Stress," *Journal of Marriage and the Family* 32, no. 2 (May 1970): 216–225.

5. Snell Putney and Gail Putney, *The Adjusted American* (New York: Harper & Row, 1964), p. 111.

6. Ibid., p. 114.

7. George Bach and Peter Wyden, *The Intimate Enemy* (New York: William Morrow, 1969), p. 6.

8. Jerold Heiss, "Degree of Intimacy and Male-Female Interaction," in *Family Roles and Interaction; An Anthology,* ed. Jerold Heiss (Chicago: Rand McNally, 1968), p. 91.

9. Lee Rainwater, "Marital Sexuality in Four Cultures of Poverty," *Journal of Marriage and the Family* 26, no. 4 (November 1964): 466.

10. These were some of the results of unpublished data collected

by the author from a sample of 284 sophomores at Michigan State University in the winter of 1969. Each of the correlation coefficients calculated was significant at the .01 level or less.

11. Betty Friedan, *The Feminine Mystique* (New York: Dell Publishing, 1963), p. 296.

12. Barrington Moore Jr., "Thoughts on the Future of the Family," in *Identity and Anxiety,* eds. Maurice Stein et al. (New York: The Free Press, 1960), p. 395.

13. Nora Scott Kinzer, "Soapy Sin in the Afternoon," *Psychology Today,* August 1973, p. 48.

14. Mervin B. Freedman, "Studies of College Alumni," in *The American College,* ed. Sanford Nevitt (New York: Wiley, 1962), p. 878.

15. De Beauvoir, *Second Sex,* p. 422; also, F. Ivan Nye and Feliz Bernardo, *The Family, Its Structure and Interaction* (New York: Macmillan, 1973), pp. 255–260.

16. Reuben Hill, *Families Under Stress* (New York: Harper and Brothers, 1949). For unpublished study, see LeMasters, *Parents,* p. 143.

17. Kingley Davis, *Human Society* (New York: Macmillan, 1949), p. 400.

18. Putney and Putney, *Adjusted American,* p. 13.

19. De Beauvoir, *Second Sex,* p. 421.

20. A. C. Kinsey et al., *Sexual Behavior in the Human Male* (Philadelphia and London: W. B. Saunders Co., 1948), p. 259 and pp. 585–588; for the more recent study, see Morton Hunt, "Sexual Behavior in the 1970s," *Playboy,* October 1973, p. 88; Virginia Satir, "Marriage as a Human-Actualizing Contract," in *The Family in Search of a Future,* ed. H. A. Otto (New York: Appleton-Century-Crofts, 1970), pp. 62–63.

21. Sebald, *Adolescence,* p. 50.

22. Talcott Parsons, "Certain Primary Sources and Patterns of Aggression in the Social Structure of the Western World," *Psychiatry* 10 (1947): 11.

23. Philip Slater, *The Pursuit of Loneliness* (Boston: The Beacon Press, 1970), p. 59.

24. U.S. Bureau of the Census, *Statistical Abstract of the United States, 1964* (Washington, D.C.: Government Printing Office, 1964), p. 65.

25. Vance Packard, *The Sexual Wilderness* (New York: David McKay, 1968), p. 376.

26. For the study of Detroit parents see Daniel Miller and Guy

Swanson, *The Changing American Parent* (New York: John Wiley, 1967), p. 215–233; for studies of marital adjustment, see W. Burgess and L. Cottrell Jr., *Predicting Success or Failure in Marriage* (New York: Prentice-Hall, 1939), p. 258–259; also, see Ernest W. Burgess and Paul Wallin, *Engagement and Marriage* (Philadelphia: J. B. Lippincott, 1953), pp. 712–713; for the project on the ratio of children per years of marriage, see John Hurley and Donna Palonen, "Marital Satisfaction and Child Density Among University Student Parents," *Journal of Marriage and the Family* 29, no. 3 (August 1967): 483–484; for marital satisfaction studies, see, for example, Robert O. Blood and Donald Wolfe, *Husbands and Wives: The Dynamics of Married Living* (Glencoe, Ill.: The Free Press, 1965), or Boyd Rollins and Harold Feldman, "Marital Satisfaction Over the Family Life Cycle," *Journal of Marriage and the Family* 31, no. 1 (January 1970): 20–27; also see Mary Hicks and Marilyn Platt, "Marital Happiness and Stability, A Review of the Research in the Sixties," *Journal of Marriage and the Family* 32, no. 4 (November 1970): 564–566.

Chapter 3

1. Bernard Berelson and Gary Steiner, *Human Behavior* (New York: Harcourt, Brace and World, 1964), p. 64.

2. Hans Sebald, *Adolescence: A Sociological Analysis* (New York: Appleton-Century-Crofts, 1968), p. 43; U.S. Office of Vital Statistics, *Vital Statistics Report*, vol. 22, no. 5 (Rockville, Md.: U.S. Department of Health, Education, and Welfare, Health Resources Administration, 25 July 1973), p. 1.

3. William Lederer and Donald Jackson, *The Mirages of Marriage* (New York: W. W. Norton, 1968), p. 13.

4. Berelson and Steiner, *Human Behavior*, p. 43.

5. U.S. Bureau of the Census, "Marital Status and Living Arrangements: March 1972," *Current Population Reports*, series P-20, no. 242 (Washington, D.C.: Government Printing Office, November 1972), p. 13.

6. Lederer and Jackson, *Mirages of Marriage*, p. 16.

7. George Levinger, "Marital Cohesiveness and Dissolution," *Journal of Marriage and the Family* 27, no. 1 (February 1965): 19–28.

8. E. E. LeMasters, *Parents in Modern America* (Homewood, Ill.: Dorsey Press, 1970), p. 149.

9. John Cuber and Peggy Harroff, *The Significant Americans* (New York: Appleton-Century-Crofts, 1965).

10. William Goode, *The Family* (Englewood Cliffs, N.J.: Prentice-Hall, 1964), p. 98; for suicide rates, see Berelson and Steiner, *Human Behavior,* p. 33.

11. Lederer and Jackson, *Mirages of Marriage,* p. 15.

12. Alvin Schorr, *Poor Kids* (New York: Basic Books, 1966), p. 16; for 1971 statistics, see U.S. Bureau of the Census, *Statistical Abstract of the United States* (Washington, D.C.: Government Printing Office, 1972), p. 39; for numbers of fatherless children, see Elizabeth Herzog and Cecelia Sudia, "Fatherless Homes," *Children* 15, no. 5 (September–October 1968): 177–182; E. E. LeMasters, *Parents,* p. 174.

13. John Belcher, "The One Parent Household; A Consequence of the Nuclear Family?" *Journal of Marriage and the Family* 29, no. 3 (August 1967): 534–540.

14. E. E. LeMasters, *Parents,* p. 160.

15. Sheldon and Eleanor Glueck, *Unraveling Juvenile Delinquency* (Cambridge: Harvard University Press, 1950), p. 91.

16. Berelson and Steiner, *Human Behavior,* p. 107.

17. Morton M. Hunt, *The World of the Formerly Married* (New York: McGraw-Hill, 1966), p. 270.

18. Ibid., p. 271.

19. Morris Rosenberg, *Society and the Adolescent Self Image* (Princeton: Princeton University Press, 1965), p. 106.

20. Bernard Farber, *Family Organization and Interaction* (San Francisco: Chandler Publishing, 1964), p. 109.

21. U.S. Bureau of the Census, *Statistical Abstract of the United States, 1972* (Washington, D.C.: Government Printing Office, 1972), p. 30.

Chapter 4

1. Ethel J. Alpenfels, "Progressive Monogamy: An Alternative Pattern," in *The Family in Search of a Future,* ed. H. A. Otto (New York: Appleton-Century-Crofts, 1970), p. 67.

2. Margaret Mead, "Marriage in Two Steps," *Redbook Magazine,* July 1966.

3. David Cooper, *The Death of the Family* (New York: Vintage Books, 1971), p. 51; Harold Greenwald, "Marriage as a Non-Legal Voluntary Association," in *The Family in Search of a Future,* ed. H. A. Otto (New York: Appleton-Century-Crofts, 1970), p. 51.

4. Lonny Myers, "Marriage, Honesty and Personal Growth," in *Renovating Marriage,* eds. Roger Libby and Robert Whitehurst (Danville, Calif.: Consensus Publications, 1973), pp. 345–359.

5. Gilbert Bartell, *Group Sex* (New York: Peter H. Wyden, 1971).

6. Robert Rimmer, "Do You, Mary, and Anne, and Beverly, and Ruth, take these men . . .," *Psychology Today,* January 1972, p. 59.

7. Edward C. Hobbs, "An Alternative Model from a Theological Perspective," in *The Family in Search of a Future,* ed. H. A. Otto (New York: Appleton-Century-Crofts, 1970), p. 40.

8. Robert Atherasion et al., "Sex," *Psychology Today* 4, no. 2 (July 1970), pp. 39–52; Larry Constantine, Joan Constantine, and Sheldon Edelman, "Group and Multilateral Relations," *The Family Coordinator* 34, no. 3 (July 1972): 268–269.

9. Gerhard Neubeck, "Polyandry and Polygyny: Viable Today?" in *The Family in Search of a Future,* ed. H. A. Otto (New York: Appleton-Century-Crofts, 1970), p. 107.

10. Constantine, Constantine, and Edelman, "Group and Multilateral Relations," p. 268; Frederick Stoller, "The Intimate Network of the Family," and Albert Ellis, "Group Marriage: A Possible Alternative?" both in *The Family in Search of a Future,* ed. H. A. Otto (New York: Appleton-Century-Crofts, 1970).

11. Ellis, "Group Marriage," p. 92–97.

12. Dean Koontz and Gerda Koontz, *The Underground Lifestyles Handbook* (Los Angeles: Aware Press, 1970), p. 29.

13. Ibid., pp. 31–33.

14. John H. Pflaum, *Delightism* (Englewood Cliffs, N.J.: Prentice-Hall, 1972), pp. 100–109.

15. Melford E. Spiro, *Kibbutz; Venture in Utopia* (New York: Schoken Books, 1963); Larry Barnett, "The Kibbutz as a Child-Rearing System: A Review of the Literature," *Journal of Marriage and the Family* 27, no. 3 (August 1965): 349.

16. B. F. Skinner, *Walden Two* (New York: Macmillan, 1948), pp. 138–141.

17. Frederick H. Stoller, "The Intimate Network of Families as a

New Structure," in *The Family in Search of a Future,* ed. H. A. Otto (New York: Appleton-Century-Crofts, 1970), pp. 145–159; *Communities* (Community Publications Cooperatives, Box 426, Louisa, Virginia, 23093); Frieda Porat, *Changing Your Life Style* (Secaucus, N.J.: Lyle Stuart, 1973), pp. 228–247.

Chapter 5

1. See, for example, Abraham Maslow, *Motivation and Personality* (New York: Harper and Brothers, 1954), pp. 116–117. Other existential writers take similar positions.

2. Richard B. Stuart, "Token Reinforcement in Marital Treatment," in *Families in Crisis,* eds. Paul Glasser and Lois Glasser (New York: Harper & Row, 1970), pp. 173–174.

3. An economic model is partly used here to help clarify the discussion. See George Homans, *Social Behavior: Its Elementary Forms* (New York: Harcourt, Brace and World, 1961), pp. 68–70.

4. Denis de Rougemont, *Love in the Western World* (Greenwich, Conn.: Fawcett Publications, 1956), p. 55.

5. Jay Haley, The Family of the Schizophrenic: A Model System," in *The Psychological Interior of the Family,* ed. G. Handel (Chicago: Aldine, 1967), pp. 271–272.

6. Ronald Mazur, "The Double Standard and People's Liberation," in *Renovating Marriage,* eds. Roger Libby and Robert Whitehurst (Danville, Calif.: Consensus Publications, 1973), p. 228.

7. Homans, *Social Behavior,* p. 55; Bernard Berelson and Gary Steiner, *Human Behavior* (New York: Harcourt, Brace and World, 1967), p. 137.

8. Thomas Harris, *I'm OK–You're OK* (New York: Harper & Row, 1967); Maslow, *Motivation and Personality,* pp. 235–260.

9. Homans, *Social Behavior,* p. 62.

Chapter 6

1. Milton Mayeroff, *On Caring* (New York: Harper & Row, 1971), pp. 44–45.

Chapter 7

1. William Goode, *World Revolution and Family Patterns* (New York: The Free Press, 1963), p. 1.

2. Ibid., p. 19.

3. Max Weber, *The Methodology of the Social Sernios* (Glencoe, Ill.: The Free Press, 1949), p. 89.

4. W. F. Ogburn and Meyer F. Nimkoff, *Technology and the Changing Family* (Boston: Houghton Miffin, 1955).

5. U.S. Bureau of the Census, *Statistical Abstract of the United States, 1971* (Washington D.C.: Government Printing Office, 1971), pp. 39 and 41.

Chapter 8

1. Snell Putney and Gail Putney, *The Adjusted American* (New York: Harper & Row, 1964), p. 12.

2. These basic human needs are outlined by such authors as Putney and Putney, *Adjusted American,* pp. 20–33; Abraham Maslow, *Motivation and Personality* (New York: Harper and Brothers, 1954), pp. 80–98; and Ashley Montagu, *On Being Human* (New York: Hawthorne Books, 1966), pp. 49–53.

3. Montagu, *On Being Human,* p. 96.

4. Erich Fromm, *The Art of Loving* (New York: Harper & Row, 1956), pp. 46–57.

5. Milton Mayeroff, *On Caring* (New York: Harper & Row, 1971), p. 30.

6. Erich Fromm, *Man for Himself* (New York: Rinehart and Company, 1947), pp. 98–101.

Chapter 9

1. Emotions are defined in many different ways. As Horace B. English and Ava C. English have pointed out in their *Comprehensive Dictionary of Psychological and Psychoanalytic Terms* (New York: Longmans, Green, 1958), it is virtually impossible as yet to define emotions without referring to several conflicting theories. The theory of Kingsley Davis suggesting that emotional manifestations are determined by social conditions and B. F. Skinner's notions suggesting that

behavior causes emotions, provide us with the following causal sequence: social conditions →behavior→emotions. Social factors thus are the independent variable. See Kingsley Davis, *Human Society* (New York: Macmillan 1948), 175–193 and B. F. Skinner, *Beyond Freedom and Dignity* (New York: Alfred A. Knopf, 1971), pp. 12–13.

2. Ronald Mazer looks at various forms of jealousy and how they add to the destructiveness of relationships. He suggests we can unlearn them and relearn more adaptive ones, in "Beyond Jealousy and Possessiveness," in *Renovating Marriage*, eds. Roger Libby and Robert Whitehurst (Danville: Consensus Publications, 1973), pp. 321–331; for an enlightening and interesting commentary on how our institutions are designed to cause us to suffer, see John H. Pflaum, *Delightism* (Englewood Cliffs, N.J.: Prentice-Hall, 1972), pp. 29–54.

3. Denis de Rougemont, *Love in the Western World* (Greenwich, Conn: Fawcett Publications, 1956), p. 219, p. 275, and p. 296.

Chapter 10

1. Abraham H. Maslow, "A Theory of Human Motivation," *Psychological Review* 50 (1943): 370–371.

2. Ibid., p. 381.

3. Samuel H. Beer, "Introduction," in *The Communist Manifesto*, Karl Marx and Friedrich Engels (New York: Appleton-Century-Crofts, 1955), p. xii.

4. Karl Marx, *Selected Works*, vol. 2 (London: L. Parsons, 1942), p. 566.

5. Jean-Paul Sartre, *Existentialism and Human Emotions* (New York: The Wisdom Library, 1957), p. 17.

6. Philip Slater, *The Pursuit of Loneliness* (Boston: Beacon Press, 1970), p. 100.

7. Ibid., pp. 117–118.

8. Albert Ellis, "Group Marriage: A Possible Alternative?" in *The Family in Search of a Future*, ed. H. A. Otto (New York: Appleton-Century-Crofts, 1970), p. 92.

Chapter 11

1. B. F. Skinner, *Beyond Freedom and Dignity* (New York: Alfred A Knopf, 1971), p. 198.

2. Philip Slater, *The Pursuit of Loneliness* (Boston: Beacon Press, 1970), p. 106.

3. Skinner, *Beyond Freedom,* p. 205.

4. Ibid., p. 215.

5. From a discussion by Phillip Slater of Jay Haley's "The Family of the Schizophrenic, A Model System," in *The Phycholocial Interior of the Family,* ed. G. Handel (Chicago: Aldine, 1967), pp. 271–272.

6. Skinner, p. 41

7. George H. Mead, *Mind, Self and Society* (Chicago: The University of Chicago Press, 1934), p. 155.

8. James F. Brennan, "Self-understanding and Social Feeling," *Journal of Individual Psychology* 23, no. 1 (May 1967): 56.

9. Ashley Montagu, *On Being Human* (New York: Hawthorn Books, 1966), p. 30.

10. See Ellen Berscheid and Elaine Walster, *Interpersonal Attraction* (Reading, Mass.: Addison-Wesley Publishing, 1969), pp. 39–40; Snell Putney and Gail Putney, *The Adjusted American* (New York: Harper & Row, 1964); Milton Mayeroff, *On Caring* (New York: Harper & Row, 1971), p. 35.

11. J. Bronowski, *Science and Human Values* (New York: Harper and Brothers, 1956), p. 27; Skinner, *Beyond Freedom,* p. 160.

12. Montagu, *On Being Human,* p. 91.

13. Slater, *Pursuit of Loneliness,* p. 8.

14. Ibid., p. 143. The word "family" has been substituted for the word "community."

15. In a recent research project I found that subjects who adorned themselves more tended to be more religious ($r=.30$), had a more authoritarian background ($r=.21$), had strong dependencies on their families ($r=.43$), were more alienated ($r=.16$), were more introverted ($r=.17$), and had less self-esteem ($r=.25$). All correlation coefficients were significant at the .01 level or less.

Epilogue

1. Theodore Roszak, *The Making of a Counter Culture* (New York: Doubleday, 1969), p. 205.

2. Herbert Feigl, "The Scientific Outlook: Naturalism and Humanism," in *Readings in the Philosophy of Science,* eds. Herbert Feigl and May Broadbeck (New York: Appleton-Century-Crofts, 1963), p. 18.

Appendix: Procedures for Establishing a Communal Family

1. Decide that you really want to try a new kind of life style where the primary bond in the group will be friendship, rather than marital or kinship ties. *Define your group as a family* right from the beginning!

2. Write a brief statement (two or three pages of four or five values which are central to your feelings about family living. These values should reflect the social functions that you expect your family to fulfill (for example, economic cooperation, child-rearing responsibilities, regulation of sexuality, emotional support, companionship). Think a lot about these values for they will become the norms of your family and will serve as the major factor in holding your family together.

3. Advertise for prospective members using your statement of values to screen them. Put an ad in the local newspaper. Attend groups whose values are similar to yours and ask to speak to the group for a few minutes about your ideas. Post statements of your intentions and values on bulletin boards. Give your phone number, and collect a list of names and phone numbers of those who call you and seem to fit into the kind of family you have in mind.

4. Set up weekly meetings to get to know these people and to discuss your interests and goals. Send out cards as reminders to those whom you are especially interested in.

5. Select five to seven people who best fit your ideas, values, and have the most in common, as the core of your family.

6. Meet regularly with these people for the purpose of designing your family structure. Meet weekly over a period of a few months to get to know each other better before you decide to move in together. Work on these problems:

   a. How will decisions be made in the family? By a consensus? By one authority? By majority? Will children have a vote?

b. What roles are necessary to create in your family? Accountant? Dietician? Secretary? Chairperson of family meetings? Coordinator of recreational activities, of household tasks, of housing? Who will fill each role? For how long?

c. How will the daily and weekly household duties be distributed? According to sex? Age? Rotated among all members? How?

d. What is acceptable sexual behavior? Monogamous marriage? Only single people in family relating either within or outside of the family? Polygamous? Only within the family? Group marriage? Only outside? Either? Will homosexuality, bisexuality, or heterosexuality be permitted?

e. What will be the living arrangements? Couples in each room? Either couples or single people in a room? Each member must have a room alone?

f. How will children be socialized? As directed by some authority figure? Adults relating to children as they desire? Control of children only by the biological parents? Determined by the whole family? Use of behavioral technology?

g. How large do you want the family to grow? How fast? Ratio of men to women? Children to adults? Blacks to whites?

h. Where do you plan to live? Urban? Rural?

i. How will the cost of food and housing be distributed among the members? Scaled according to income? According to size of room and amount each member eats? Equal for all?

j. How will new members be admitted? By consensus? After going through some screening process? What will be the process?

7. Assign roles to members and have the secretary start a notebook of family codes. Include a statement of family values and objectives, of roles and role-obligations, and of the decision-making process. Include also all other decisions made by the family.

8. Find a large house which best fits your needs and move in.

9. Keep the structure as flexible as possible. Everything won't work the way you planned. Be ready to make changes if you want your new family to last!

Good luck!

Bibliography

New Perspectives

Reich, Charles. *The Greening of America.* New York: Random House, 1970.
Roszak, Theodore. *The Making of a Counter Culture.* New York: Doubleday, 1969.
Slater, Philip. *The Pursuit of Loneliness.* Boston: Beacon Press, 1970.
Toffler, Alvin. *Future Shock.* New York: Random House, 1970.

Interpersonal Relations

Crosby, John F. *Illusion and Disillusion: The Self in Love and Marriage.* Belmont: Wadsworth, 1973.
O'Neil, Nena, and George O'Neil. *Open Marriage.* New York: M. Evans, 1972.
Putney, Snell, and Gail Putney. *The Adjusted American.* New York: Harper & Row, 1964.
Rogers, Carl. *On Becoming a Person.* Boston: Houghton Mifflin, 1961.
Slater, Philip. "On Social Regression," *American Sociological Review,* 28 (June 1963), 351–359.

Sexuality

Hunt, Morton. "Sexual Behavior in the 1970s," *Playboy* (October 1973).
Millar, Mervyn. "Apollonians and Dionepians: Some Impressions of Sex in the Counter Culture," in *Renovating Marriage,* eds. Roger Libby and Robert Whitehurst. Danville, Calif.: Consensus Publications, 1973.
Sprey, Jetze. "On the Institutionalization of Sex," *Journal of Marriage and Family* (August 1969).

Multiple Mating

Constantine, Larry, and Joan Constantine. "Group and Multilateral Relations," *The Family Coordinator,* 21 (July 1972).

Denfield, Duane, and Michael Gordon. "Mate Swapping: The Family That Swings Together Clings Together," *Journal of Sex Research,* 7 (May 1967).

Ellis, Albert. "Group Marriage: A Possible Alternative," in *The Family in Search of a Future,* ed. Herbert A. Otto. New York: Appleton-Century-Crofts, 1970.

Rimmer, Robert. *The Harrad Experiment.* New York: New American Library, 1968.

Varni, Charles A. "Contexts of Conversion: The Case of Swinging," in *Renovating Marriage,* eds. Roger Libby and Robert Whitehurst. Danville, Calif.: Consensus Publications, 1973.

Conceptions of Love

Beigel, Hugo. "Romantic Love," *American Sociological Review,* 14 (June 1951).

Benoit, Hubert. *The Many Faces of Love.* New York: Pantheon Books, 1955.

Cappelanus, Andreas. *The Art of Courtly Love.* New York: Frederick Ungar, 1957.

Goode, William. "The Theoretical Importance of Love," *American Sociological Review,* 24 (February 1959).

Foote, Nelson. "Love," *Psychiatry,* 16 (August 1953).

Fromm, Erich. *The Art of Loving.* New York: Harper & Row, 1956.

Prescott, Daniel. "The Role of Love in Human Development," *Journal of Home Economics,* 44 (1952).

Sullivan, Harry Stack. *Conceptions of Modern Psychiatry.* Washington D.C.: William Alanson White Psychiatric Foundation, 1947.

Winch, Robert. *Mate Selection.* New York: Harper and Brothers, 1958.

Toward a New Morality

Feigl, Herbert. "The Scientific Outlook: Naturalism and Humanism," in *Readings in the Philosophy of Science,* eds. Herbert Feigl and

May Broadbeck. New York: Appleton-Century-Crofts, 1963.

Mead, George H. *Mind, Self and Society.* Chicago: University of Chicago Press, 1934.

Montagu, Ashley, *On Being Human.* New York: Hawthorn Books, 1966.

Piaget, Jean. *The Moral Judgement of the Child.* New York: Free Press, 1965.

Skinner, B. F. *Beyond Freedom and Dignity.* New York: Knopf, 1971.

Thamm, Robert. "Self-autonomy, Consistency and Intersystemic Involvement." Unpublished doctoral dissertation, Michigan State University, 1968.

Index